Identifying Children with Special Needs: A Practical Guide to Developmental Screening

Lee Marvin Joiner, PhD

Professor of Special Education
Southern Illinois University, Carbondale

LEARNING PUBLICATIONS

Learning Publications, Inc.
P.O. Box 1326
Holmes Beach, Florida 33509

Library of Congress Catalog Card Number 78-58531

ISBN 0-918452-14-7

Printing: 1 2 3 4 5 6 7 8   Year: 8 9 0 1 2

Printed in the United States of America

*Dedicated
to
Lotte Kaliski*

ACKNOWLEDGEMENTS

The author wishes to acknowledge the contributions of the many classroom teachers and colleagues who have worked to meet the needs of all children and in doing so originated many of the ideas and practices described in the present volume.

Thanks is extended to Drs. Robert Stoneburner and James Teska of Southern Illinois University and Dr. Robert Carpenter, Director of the Southwest Illinois University Regional Special Education Association for their constructive comments and criticisms. Dr. Carpenter helped develop many of the ideas, materials, and practices described in the chapter, "Building Community Awareness."

Issues relating to the use of children's drawings as developmental indices were brought to the attention of the author by Dr. Edward Dieffenbach. And Ms. Carol Williams provided valuable research assistance. To these persons the author is indebted.

PREFACE

Identifying children's special needs and providing remedial programs have been generally accepted as the responsibility of elementary and secondary educators. Recently, however, an emphasis has been placed on preventive education and one of the current priorities of the U.S. Office of Education is to encourage schools to provide more extensive and improved early education programs for the handicapped.

With the downward extension of special needs assessment into the preschool population has arisen a need for the co-involvement of other community professionals such as social workers, family physicians, public health nurses, and family service agency personnel in the identification of children with special needs. This movement is consistent with a reorganization of professional thought concerning how to serve children with special needs. The general direction of movement is away from specialization and toward a system of shared responsibility. Special needs are no longer considered the concern of special educators alone.

The contemporary broadening of expectations within many professions to include identifying children with special needs, regardless of one's professional function in the human service area, has arisen from:

1. Judicial decisions which define new obligations for communities and schools toward special needs children.

2. Federal and state legislation which requires that schools provide "child-find" or "identification" programs and compensatory programs for meeting children's special needs.

3. A changing social philosophy which assigns the community broader responsibilities for the welfare of all it's members, regardless of the type or extent of their human service needs.

The present volume is concerned with practical and effective procedures for identifying children's special needs. It is assumed that identification of special needs will be a joint effort involving general educators, parents, and those traditionally concerned with the education and treatment of the handicapped. Only the first element in the service continuum is examined here: developmental screening. Developmental screening is the first step in an effective community program for detecting and meeting the extraordinary or "special needs" of children.

TABLE OF CONTENTS

1

Identifying Special
Needs Children

Today there is a general awareness, among both laymen
and professionals, of the many handicapping conditions that
require special community and educational services. But despite an increasing awareness of the nature of the problem, a
large number of children in need of special services still await
help. These are the unidentified children whose special needs,
if they remain undetected, may hinder their educational performance and later functioning as productive members of
their communities. According to estimates by the U.S. Office
of Education, only 55% of the nation's 7,800,000 handicapped
and special needs learners are receiving appropriate educational services. The remaining 45% are "unserved" or "under-
served." (National Advisory Committee on the Handicapped,
1976)

The following population statistics prepared by the U.S. Office of Education reveal the number of children by handicapping condition who could benefit from a comprehensive "identification" effort and follow-up services (National Advisory Committee on the Handicapped, 1976):

Handicapping Condition	Total (est.)	Unserved
Speech Impaired	2,200,000	73,000
Mentally Impaired	1,500,000	157,000
Learning Disabled (severe)	1,900,000	1,706,000
Emotionally Disturbed	1,300,000	1,055,000
Physically Impaired	328,000	73,000
Deaf	49,000	4,000
Hard of Hearing	328,000	262,000
Multihandicapped	40,000	24,000

For children under five years of age, the situation is especially serious. Among this age group there are an estimated 1,100,000 children with handicaps and special needs, 682,000 of whom are receiving no appropriate educational assistance. The existence of a high proportion of unidentified young handicapped children is especially unfortunate because it is believed that these are the children who could most benefit from "preventive" teaching.

Educators and those who establish social policy agree that the number of inadequately served special needs learners can and should be reduced. A fundamental tactic for more adequately distributing service according to need is to upgrade the competencies of teachers and other professionals involved with children for detecting evidence of special need. One method of proceeding toward the goal of full service for children in need is to initiate systematic, high quality identification programs which would locate children who would benefit from special services, educational or health.

THE NEED TO SCREEN EARLY

Good screening programs detect problems early and if learning impediments are detected early in the school career of the child, or better yet at the pre-school level, there is a greater likelihood of preventing "cumulative effects." Cumulative effects occur when children begin to fail important developmental tasks because of unmet special needs and each successive failure decreases the likelihood that new skills will be learned. In essence the child learns to be less able that he originally was. In a very short time, often by the age of eight years, the child reaches a point where cumulative effects interfere with his or her ability to profit from even remedial or compensatory programs. And much "unlearning" must occur before the child can be reached.

A second reason for early screening is that sensory-motor deficits are commonly involved in learning problems. Sensory-motor skills are "readiness" skills and young children respond well to systematic practice in these areas. While older children may experience sensory-motor deficits, older children are often less cooperative in remedial drills, being unwilling to practice movements and exercises which they see as being too immature. Sensory motor skills also are "trainable" in that good gains can usually be observed with instruction. Visible progress serves as incentive to both teacher and student for further effort.

A third advantage of early screening is that if special needs are detected and if special programs are initiated, these programs will have a longer potential lifetime than if screening were to be conducted at higher grade levels. Pre-school screening allows educators to develop programs addressed to the child's needs from the day kindergarten is entered.

The importance which has become attached to early identification in order to permit early intervention is further recognized in the policy statements of the National Advisory Committee on the Handicapped (1976). In the words of the Committee:

> Research has clearly documented that early intervention into the education of handicapped children is of critical importance in enabling such youngsters not only to make greater progress as learners but to become participating members of society.

And on this basis the National Advisory Committee made the following recommendations:

> That the Governors and legislatures of the several states join forces in making sure that educational services are authorized, and provided, for every handicapped child in their states, beginning at the child's birth, and that the Commissioner of Education lend his active support to the achievement of this goal.

THE DEVELOPMENTAL SCREENING PROCESS

The first step in identifying children with handicaps and/or special needs is "developmental screening." Developmental screening is really nothing new and mysterious because to some degree parents and teachers have always done this. They have watched children mature and consciously or unconsciously compared what they observed with some standard. Their standard for comparison may have been derived from direct experiences with other children they have observed growing up or from what they have read or been taught. When people carefully observe a child's physical, social, and mental maturation and compare what they see with some standard, they are engaging in simple, informal, developmental screening.

While it would be ideal for all parents to be able to recognize signs of special need among their children and thus serve as screening agents, it is an unrealistic expectation. Teachers, on the other hand, are expected to demonstrate competence in child development and can be expected to learn to recognize the significance of at least some of the basic early warning signs of special need. The legitimacy of this expectation arises from the unique position of the teacher as an observer of child growth and their professional training and social role. All children spend a major portion of their childhood in the presence of teachers.

In a society with increasing paternalism, professionalization and role differentiation, parents have become conditioned to rely upon outside experts to assume a helping role in many aspects of their personal lives. And when parents observe something that is troubling them about their child's development, many of them seek advice from teachers. Less advantaged parents and those in rural areas are especially likely to rely on teachers rather than physicians or other professionals for advice on parenting.

In addition to being expected to respond adequately to the questions that parents pose, teachers are usually the first "experts" in child development to interact with a child on an extended basis. So for many parents, the teacher functions as a surrogate when it comes to detecting special needs. But in order to detect special needs and problems before they escalate into major crises, teachers need an understanding of what and how to observe. What are the early signs of handicaps or special need? When, and how should formal screening be conducted? Should commercially available instruments be used and if so which ones?

PROBLEMS CAUSED BY
LACK OF SCREENING PROVISIONS

Beyond the fact that teachers are not always fully prepared to assist in planning or conducting developmental screening programs, the absence of carefully planned, formal screening provisions in a school district tends to decrease the likelihood that teachers will voluntarily seek assistance from resource persons when they suspect that a child may manifest extraordinary or special needs. Without a specific screening assignment, teachers may be reluctant to report difficulties that children are experiencing that may be indicative of special need. Their reluctance to seek resource assistance or "refer" a child may stem from a fear that revealing the existence of a problem might jeopardize their competence rating in the eyes of their supervisors. There is an often expressed fear that teachers with higher rates of "referral" may be viewed as less competent than those teachers who maintain a lower profile and manage "to handle" all students assigned them.

Probably the connotation that teachers who refer children for diagnosis or closer study are inadequate is a result of misinformation about or a lack of awareness of current insights into teaching the special needs child. Adequate programming for the special needs child includes the expectation that additional allocations of resources and personnel are necessary to the achievement of good educational progress. Special needs must be met with carefully designed compensatory programs; to meet all children's special needs would be beyond the capacity of the best general classroom teachers if they were functioning unaided.

The author has observed, repeatedly, that teachers' reluctance to become involved in the search for children with special needs is greatly reduced when school systems establish "formal" developmental screening programs along with inservice training. When formal screening programs exist, it becomes routinely accepted that some children will manifest special needs and require follow-up services that are beyond the capacity of the general teacher to provide. Noting and reporting patterns of atypical growth and adjustment then become accepted job functions of teachers.

The concept of special needs should convey to educators the expectations that all children should be examined to determine their special strengths and problems areas. However, not all children need to be referred to school psychologists and other specially trained educators for extensive diagnoses. That would be beyond the resources of nearly any school and would contribute to the inefficient use of resource staff and the time available for teaching.

What is needed is to use the most valid screening procedures and instruments available for identifying those children who should have more intensive diagnostic services.

There should be no doubt about the advantages of a properly conducted screening program. A well organized screening program will help teachers, support staff, and administrators as they, in turn, attempt to help their students.

SCREENING AND THE REFERRAL SYSTEM

How do the schools generally go about locating special needs children? In most school systems there exists some kind of referral system. While there are many differences in the way referral systems operate, nearly all referral systems establish procedures for teachers to refer children with suspected needs so that certain children may be more closely examined by school psychologists and other professionals. In a referral system, screening includes all those activities used by parents and teachers to decide whether or not to recommend a child for more intensive examination.

One of the reasons that large numbers of children with special needs are not referred is that educators often do not know all of the many signs indicating various needs. In addition, educators are often unaware that there are inexpensive procedures and instruments for detecting those who should be referred for more extensive examination. To complicate the problem further, many educators are not in a position to weigh the strengths and weaknesses of the various screening procedures and instruments available to them. As a consequence, all they can do is go by the claims of test publishers and consultants — which are often exaggerated.

AN OVERVIEW OF THIS BOOK

It is important to successful school programming to be able to identify with reasonable accuracy the characteristics and special needs of students. If assessments of children are not made with some reasonable degree of accuracy, continuing problems are likely to be experienced by the staff, the children, and the children's parents.

In order to detect special needs before they escalate into problems, educators usually need resources, instruments and instructions in their use. They need to know how to detect the signs of special need. They also need to know when to make their assessments. And when instruments or tests are used, educators need to have considerable understanding of their limitations. They need to know when and when not to use them. They need to know the appropriateness of any screening instrument they employ.

To aid in meeting these professional needs, this book:

- provides information and recommendations relating to designing special needs screening programs for children, before and after school entry.

• provides descriptive information concerning the large number of instruments available for use in screening programs.

• provides standards and procedures that can be used by professionals in judging the suitability of instruments for local applications.

2
The Meaning of Screening

Much of the literature regarding those identification or assessment activities engaged in under the term "screening" are unclear as to their unique meanings, and if distinct, how they are related. For our purposes it is unnecessary to be too concerned over what is the best definition of terms. However, we need to be sensitive to four distinct kinds of activities that are carried out in screening programs.

BASIC PROCESSES OF SCREENING

Rather simply, the four basic features or processes of a screening program involve:

- the observation process;

- the process of assembling of observations;

- the process of drawing conclusions from the assembled observations; and

- the placement recommendation process which, where necessary, includes referrals of students for more extensive diagnostic study.

The Observation Process

The observation process can be either formal, informal or both. That is, observations may be formally made by using structured testing procedures, or they may be informally made by teachers without following specified procedures for making observations. In the latter case, a teacher, for example, may note that a student is unable to pronounce certain consonant sounds or that she lacks the language syntax she expected of children the student's age. Regardless of whether or not observations are formally structured or informal, it is important that they be both accurate and representative of a fairly broad range of student behavior.

A well thought-out screening program usually provides a *systematic* procedure for making observations. This will often involve the establishment of policies which prescribe the use of certain tests and inventories for the more informal observations of teachers, parents, and where appropriate, the direct observation of students. The opposite of systematic observation procedures is to be haphazard—no sound basis for educational practice.

The Process of Assembling Observations

Even if one has acquired a set of valid and useful data which was systematically gained, the data will be of little value if it is so disorganized that one is unable to draw useful conclusions about children.

As part of the screening process, observational data is recorded and stored in a way that will be useful for professionals. Systematic assembling of screening data promotes efficiency at the diagnostic level because diagnosticians can depend on the availability of certain basic information and design their diagnostic approaches accordingly. If with each child who is referred for detailed diagnostic workup a different set of information appears, valuable diagnostic time is wasted in interpreting this preliminary information.

The Drawing of Conclusions

In addition to being systematic, making and presenting useful observations of children, screening programs detect broad signs of handicapping conditions, learning impediments or special talents. Unlike a diagnostic program which attempts to discover the exact type, extent, and cause of a child's problem or special needs, a screening program only leads to conclusions that for certain children "something may be wrong," and that these children need to be referred for further diagnosis, or that they are "at risk."

The Placement Recommendation Process

However, screening provides "inconclusive evidence." In fact we expect that a substantial proportion, often about twenty percent, of the children showing broad signs of handicapping conditions, learning impediments or special talents at screening will be later diagnosed as having no major deficits. In the language of assessment, children who show broad signs of handicapping conditions or learning impediments at screening but who later in the diagnostic phase show little or no evidence of serious disorders are termed "false positives." In other words, screening has suggested that a problem might exist but more careful study has indicated this to be false.

But no matter how sophisticated or elaborate the screening program, some children with real problems will remain undisclosed. Because some children with special needs are missed by screening programs, provisions are needed to continue screening observations of children by teachers and other staff. The fact that a child has "passed" screening at one time provides no guarantee that handicaps or learning impediments are absent or will not develop. Teachers should remember this important limitation of screening and not fall victim to the belief that all children who "pass" screening lack problems.

Remember, screening activities are the first steps in locating children with special needs. Furthermore, these first steps must be repeated; screening activities need to be repeated during the child's school career. But because early intervention is important in preventing handicapping conditions from producing secondary deficits, such as school failure or social maladjustment, screening programs for pre-school and kindergarten children have received the most attention recently.

WHAT SCREENING DOESN'T MEAN

Educators have devoted a considerable amount of time and energy to the pursuit of terms to describe somewhat exactly the conditions that they deal with, often changing terms and their own educational practices. For example, at different times they used the terms educationally "subnormal," "mentally handicapped," "morons," "mentally retarded," and "developmentally disabled" to refer to the same population. Some of these terminology problems result from changing fads and fashions within the educational community and some result from insights gained regarding the negative connotations and surplus meanings of the terms we use. Also, new and unintended meanings have a way of arising spontaneously when laymen begin borrowing professional terms for use in everyday discourse.

In the present book the term "screening" is used because it is generally familiar to educators. In using the term screening, however, it is recognized that some negative connotations have already emerged. In the common language, for instance, "screening" can mean excluding undesirable persons from situations, groups or opportunities. "Screening" may also refer, in certain situations, to separating out defective or undesirable individuals.

In view of these possibly negative connotations, to which the public may respond, it may be argued that it is better to use some other equivalent term such as "identification" when communicating with laymen about screening programs. Otherwise, some of the negative connotations of the term "screening" may result in parent resistance or incomplete cooperation in the kinds of programs that will be described in later chapters.

SCREENING DOESN'T EXPLAIN DIFFERENCES

Because the basic goal of screening is to identify children with learning impediments and special needs that may hinder their later educational development, there is danger that teachers and other professionals may attribute all variations in learning to individual differences. When we screen, we seem to be saying that it's something about the child that is responsible for school problems, something intrinsic to him/her.

But this is an inaccurate conclusion. There is considerable evidence to indicate that many school learning problems can be attributed to trivial or dull curriculum, poor instruction, personality conflicts with teachers, and the general ecology of the classroom. (Adelman, 1970) While these instructional and situational variables could be examined and taken into consideration, narrow approaches to screening which involve only tests tend to ignore them. Taken alone, screening tests provide us with clues concerning which children are most likely to be adversely affected by these conditions, regardless of the degree to which they exist within the life of an individual child. Many of the inaccuracies associated with screening result from failing to include instructional variables or social context variables in our prediction model.

A further danger of adopting the view that all explanations of performance differences are to be found within children and therefore revealed by tests is that teacher expectancies may become influenced by information obtained in screening. The teacher might reason that those children "failing" screening are likely to experience learning problems because of the nature of "their condition." This hypothesis about the future development of the child helps shape the teacher's perceptions and conclusions concerning the adequacy of the child's daily performance as it emerges. Educators have termed this phenomenon as "self-fulfilling prophecy."

3

Screening and
the Community

Two basic concerns face all educators as they go about
planning and conducting their programs for students. One is
the law and the other is the attitude of the public and other
educators toward what they are attempting. These concerns
are particularly relevant when it comes to the development of
new programs such as screening.

SCREENING AND THE LAW

Since the 1960's there has been mounting pressure to
provide for universal and systematic early identification and
compensatory programming for children with special needs.
Whereas formerly, schools were free to determine whether or
not and the extent to which they wished to become involved
in the identification of children with special needs, today
schools are required to provide identification programs if they
wish to receive certain federal educational assistance funds.

Providing for the identification of children with special needs and/or handicaps is no longer optional for states and school districts.

In response to the fact that many of the special needs children in America remain unidentified and unserved, Congress formulated *Public Law 94-142*. This legislation, educators agree, has important implications for school practices. Scheduled for full implementation in 1978, the *Education for All Handicapped Children Act* sets forth national policy stating that all handicapped persons have a fundamental right to an appropriate education.

Widely acclaimed as a "Bill of Rights" for the handicapped, this legislation requires that a free public education be made available to all handicapped children between the ages of 3 and 18 by no later than September of 1978. By 1980, these requirements will extend to ages 3 to 21 unless state attendance laws exempt 3 − 5 and 18 − 21 age brackets.

To achieve a full educational service goal for the handicapped, P. L. 94-142 authorizes a massive expansion of federal funds to be distributed to local education agencies through grants programs. Starting with a congressional authorization for 387 million dollars in FY 1978, stepwise increases each fiscal year will result in a maximum authorization of 3.16 billion dollars for FY 1982.

Although the magnitude of authorized funding is a dramatic feature of the legislation, of equal importance is that unlike other Federal education laws, P. L. 94-142 is to be considered permanent; it has no expiration date. Also, it should be carefully noted that the policies articulated in the law are binding regardless of the levels of appropriation that are forthcoming. Educators must understand these policies;

they will have a significant impact on the organization of school services for the handicapped and the duties of special and general educators, particularly those pertaining to identification or screening.

A congressional finding which relates to screening for special needs and which served as a basis for the Education for All Handicapped Children Act was:

> Developments in the training of teachers and in diagnostic and instructional procedures and methods have advanced to the point that given appropriate funding, State and local educational agencies can and will provide effective special education and related services to meet the needs of handicapped children.

One of the requirements that local school districts must meet in order to receive payments under P. L. 94-142 is that they:

 . . . provide that all children residing within the jurisdiction of the local education agency who are handicapped, regardless of severity, will be:

- identified,
- located,
- evaluated.

Clearly, Congress believed that American educators were prepared to conduct screening to identify children with special needs, that adequate procedures and professional expertise existed in the field, and that local schools could respond effectively to childrens' special needs if the financial means were provided.

While Public Law 94-142 requires that "handicapped" children be identified, the author has chosen to use the term "special needs," a concept which is inclusive of the handicapped but broader. The concept "special needs" carries with it the connotation that something positive can and should be done by the schools to follow up with preventive or remedial education provisions. Too often the concept "handicapped" has caused professionals to focus on the limitations of individuals so described. Curricula have often been "watered down" in response to the child's "handicaps" or professionals have adopted the view that only very limited goals and outcomes are to be expected from these individuals. Also, the term "handicap" tends to focus more attention on the individual and his disorder than on the community's responsibility for meeting the needs of all children regardless of the severity of the problem.

RESISTENCE TO SCREENING

Despite mounting pressure by state and federal authorities for school districts to locate children with special needs or handicaps, effective screening programs remain lacking in some school systems. Why should schools resist locating children who can benefit from special services? A study by the National Education Project revealed one of the facts that accounts for this resistence.

At the present time, providing educational services for children identified as having special needs costs about 2.4 times as much per pupil as do general education programs.

Today, many school districts are experiencing financial problems and see programs for special needs learners as competing
with general education funding needs. When this happens,
teachers feel pressured to refer children for diagnostic evaluations only when absolutely necessary; usually after problems
have reached crisis proportions. Formal programs of screening
leading to preventive interventions are thought to identify
excessive numbers of children needing special services. Once
identified, schools are required by law to provide services for
children with special needs and handicaps.

A major controversy surrounding the provision of special education services for the "handicapped" and consequent-
ly for any efforts at identifying individuals with special needs,
has been the social and educational consequences of being
officially identified as "deviant." Erikson (1957) said,
"whenever a psychiatrist makes the clinical diagnosis of an
existing need for treatment, society makes the social diagnosis of a changed status of one of its members." This phenomenon is at the heart of one of the major problems faced by
those responsible for establishing developmental screening
programs: how to gain insight, as early as possible, into a
child's special needs without subjecting him to damaging side
effects.

Typically, in "differential diagnosis," educators and
school psychologists have sought clusters of observable behavioral or genetic characteristics which could serve as a basis
for educational groupings; the idea behind this being that
children who show traits or characteristics can be provided
with a common instructional package which is most relevant
to their needs.

One of the major criticisms of this traditional approach to identification and diagnosis is that as a consequence of these activities, children were sorted out, labelled, and assigned to separate, often segregated school programs whose effectiveness was open to challenge. Part of the educational problem resulting from "diagnosis" was thought to be that classifying children according to various "disability" criteria resulted in destructive "self-fulling prophesies." The diagnostic label provided an explanation for the child's failure to learn at an average rate or for socially maladaptive behavior.

It was noted in the professional literature that teachers react toward "handicapped" children according to preconceived expectations based on stereotypes which are socio-cultural in origin rather than reacting directly to the children's needs on a rational, productive basis. In teacher training programs, Salvia, Clark and Ysseldyke (1973) noted that both prospective regular class and special class teachers retained socio-cultural stereotypes of children labelled gifted, normal, and retarded. In all instances, they found that the "retarded" children were rated less favorably than the "normal" or "gifted."

Diagnostic labels are especially dangerous if people close to the child see the child in terms of the label and, if then, the child begins to behave in a manner consistent with these expectations. Towne and Joiner (1968) argued that the meanings of diagnostic labels actually expanded beyond the behaviors that were used as a basis for defining the diagnostic category. The likelihood was that the child to whom a diagnostic label had been attached would be viewed as personally, intrinsically defective rather than someone with special needs that could and ought to be met by the schools and other community agencies.

> Thus, whatever the label means to others, regardless of its accuracy or connection with the child's immediate behavior, each person's expectations and interpretations of the child's behavior will be affected by his definition of what this kind of person is supposed to be like. Vague feelings and observations about the child's behavior become anchored to the label. A social object is created by developing a cognitive category which connects many disparate characteristics. And the social object is " authenticated" since the observed behaviors are defined as causal conditions in explaining the behavior. Thus, the student's inept performance of an important task will be explained by defining him as a member of a subset who is supposed to behave that way by definition.

Not only teachers, but parents and other individuals who interact with the child responded to the diagnostic label. As suggested by Kelly (1974), when labels supplant the actual behaviors of a child to the point where the child begins to be seen as an object to be tested and programmed we have, in essence, engaged in a dehumanizing process.

Serious confrontations ultimately emerged over the entire process of differential diagnosis, aptitude, and achivement testing, particularly in instances where the diagnostic process led to differential educational programming. According to Ross, DeYoung and Cohen (1971), those who challenged the appropriateness and legality of these programs claimed:

- The instruments used were inadequate and failed to measure actual learning abilities.

- Persons administering the tests were too often untrained or incompetent.

- Parents had little control over what happened subsequent to assessment.

- Evidence of socio-cultural biases in the instruments were abundant.

Many positive steps have been taken to remedy these inequities but much remains to be done before any full resolution is achieved. Rather than abandoning the entire diagnostic process, schools have moved in the direction of assessments that are directed toward revealing exactly what the child can and cannot perform, a more behavioral approach which concentrates on the observable manifestations of a disorder rather than on the underlying etiology. With this approach, test results are more directly translatable into remedial programming.

Rather than providing special segregated classes for children with similar diagnostic profiles, interventions have been tailored according to the concept of "least restrictive alternative." What this means is that the first goal of education programs is to treat the child's problem within the normal social environment that children experience, the regular classroom. Interactions which cause a child to be removed from the normal social experiences of growing up in the community in the same way that the average child does are considered "restrictive" to some degree. A very restrictive environment would be a residential, institutional placement. A less restrictive intervention would be to provide supplementary or "resource" services that give special assistance, on a one-to-one basis, to support a child and help guarantee his success in a normal school program.

Tremendous gains have been made in providing for parent involvement in any educational placement decisions, testing, and classification activities. School records are open for parent inspection and parents have the right to challenge the accuracy or relevance of any items contained therein. States have adopted school codes which spell out in detail the "due process" which is available to parents should they fail to agree with diagnostic decisions. Parents are entitled to be informed of and involved in every step that is taken regarding their child's educational experience.

Competencies of those who administer tests are being upgraded through in-service programs and through teacher education programs which have responded with sensitivity to the above issues. Many new instruments are becoming available for "screening" which can be competently administered by teachers and paraprofessionals who have limited backgrounds in psychometrics.

4

Screening and School Programming

Whenever educators consider the values and limitations of screening, it is important that they be fully aware of the implications of screening for:

- the severity of their student's problems;

- placing their students in programs;

- developing individualized instruction;

- the heterogenous makeup of their student bodies; and

- the making of final decisions about the nature of student needs.

SCREENING AND THE
SEVERITY OF STUDENT PROBLEMS

The more severe the disorder the greater the likelihood that the disorder will be detected while the child is very young and without benefit of a formal screening program. Children who are deaf, blind, psychotic, or profoundly retarded usually reveal physical differences or extreme behaviors which usually, but not always, alert physicians and parents to the presence of serious problems. Then problems are often referred to as *low incidence* handicapped conditions. Figure 1 portrays their relative distribution in a population.

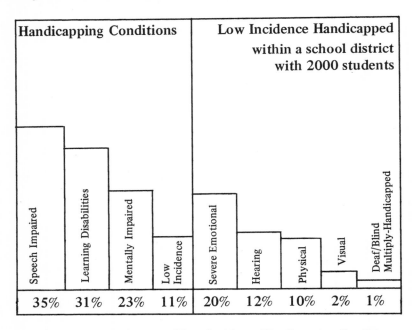

Figure 1: Distribution of Low Incidence Handicapping Conditions.
From materials provided by the Southwest Illinois Regional Special Education Association.

However, as is so often true when considering generalizations about human differences, there are enough important exceptions to prevent us from excluding the severely impaired from our attention in a screening program. Not all children with severe learning impediments will be identified by parents and physicians without the aid of a formal effort of some kind at the community level. Dissemination of information concerning the early warning signs of handicaps and special needs is one of the major ways that schools contribute to the identification of children with severe disorders. These methods will be described later in the book.

If good community awareness programs exist, the primary concern of the schools is for detecting mild learning impediments. These are the conditions which so often go unnoticed until cumulative effects become evident in the middle or upper elementary grades. For these unidentified children, regular classroom teachers represent the primary service providers and it is therefore important that these professionals fully understand the screening process.

SCREENING IS NOT FOR PLACEMENT

Educators (Maitland, Nadeau, and Nadeau, 1974) have been interested in the "timing" of screening test administration, seeking to determine at what point during the school year the most effective use of screening data may be achieved. The reason for their interest in the "timing" of screening is that when screening is conducted late in the school year, results are more often used to support placement decisions than to initiate detailed diagnostic follow-up. In their survey of how screening results were used, they found that approximately 50% - 60% of the schools surveyed were using screening test results for determining the educational placement of children.

Taken alone, however, most screening instruments yield data that is inadequate to support placement decisions. Screening data should only comprise a small portion of the evidence used in making such judgements. Most screening tests are psychometrically weak; they lack sufficient precision to justify their use as sole determiners of events with such important long-term consequences as type of educational placement. Screening provides rough indications of the presence of a problem, handicap, or special need. Screening tells us little about the exact nature of a problem nor does screening provide us with extensive suggestions about how a problem might be amerliorated. Educational placement is in reality a "treatment" and there is no evidence that screening devices provide us with enough evidence of sufficient quality to support treatment decisions.

SCREENING AND INDIVIDUALIZED INSTRUCTION

A complaint of teachers who receive assessment results from school psychologists is that too often test results have few direct implications for planning individual instruction. If information fails to provide direct aid in planning, some teachers view the activities that produced it as uneconomical, superfluous, or unnecessary. How legitimate is this complaint in the case of screening?

Screening tentatively suggests the possible presence of a risk condition of special need. Lacking more detailed follow-up observations and testing, screening results can be expected to provide information of only limited value in the planning of instruction. We must remember that the basic purpose of screening is to help identify children who are "at risk." And we must be careful to avoid expecting too much of screening and thereby becoming jaded, condemning the process because it fails to provide information which is actually outside its intended purpose.

As will be described in later sections of the book, there are a number of different types of screening devices which vary in quality, scope, complexity, length, detail, and structure. Some appear more closely correlated with the instructional program than others. But to select screening devices or methods on the basis of their apparent relevance to individual instruction planning is to ignore the main question: "How well does the screening device identify children with special needs?

ONE SCREENING PROGRAM FOR ALL?

In examining large populations for the presence of physical disorders, a single instrument or technique is commonly used. For example, screening for the presence of phenylketonuria involves an analysis of the infant's urine, a test which is relevant to all infants. In comparison to screening for physical disorders such as phenylketonuria, turberculosis, syphilis, and so forth, screening for handicaps or special needs is difficult and complicated. Not only are the conditions for which we screen less well defined, the same screening techniques are not equally suitable for all children.

Because a child's performance is a product not only of his abilities and personality, but also the social context in which he learns and the organization of the curriculum, instruction, and classroom, screening should ideally be adjusted according to some of these factors. For example, a major dilemma faced by educators today is that many children who are of Latino ethnicity cannot be adequately examined by tests or procedures which were designed for monolingual Anglo children. Even Spanish translations of tests can be inadequate because some concepts differ cross-culturally. Questions of which child is ready and which is "at risk" have little meaning unless considered within the context of the social-cultural-linguistic situation in which the child must function and in terms of the expectancies defined for him. (Adelman, 1971)

SCREENING NEEDS TO BE CONTINUOUS

Many school systems take pride in having excellent formal screening programs. Their staffs are well trained and their procedures seem to be the best possible. Parents cooperate and the community is involved.

Yet even when excellence exists, the overall effectiveness of such screening programs may be limited by a failure to make formal provisions for repeated screening. A single time or age for screening is unlikely to be effective for detecting special needs. For example, most learning disabilities remain undetectable until the child reaches the third or fourth grade level. In the physical area, hearing or vision problems can appear at any time.

Like a physical examination, good screening cannot be implemented at a single age or grade level and then forgotten. At least some forms of screening will need to be conducted on a repetitive basis.

5

Planning a
Screening Program

Planning a screening program for a school or school system is a mutual challenge for administrators, teachers, school psychologists, consultants, and community representatives. Important decisions must be made during the planning and design stage, decisions which will result in major differences among communities in the kinds of screening programs offered. This chapter describes some of the issues involved in arriving at these decisions. It is meant to aid persons involved in planning by providing them with a frame of reference for approaching the problem.

MAJOR QUESTIONS

- Will all children of a given age or grade be screened?

- Will the same screening procedures be used with each child?

●   Will simple or complex assessments be used?

●   When will screening be conducted?

COMPREHENSIVE OR SELECTIVE SCREENING?

A "comprehensive" screening program is one which is targeted to a single age group or grade level and which insures that all children of that age or grade within a school district are assessed. Comprehensive screening programs are typically formal. A special time and location is assigned for screening, and complete participation by teachers, children, and sometimes parents is expected.

"Selective" screening is concerned with a group of children that has been previously delimited. Parents, physicians, social workers, school psychologists, or teachers initiate the process for each individual case on the basis of informally acquired evidence of special need that results from their daily or routine contacts with a particular child. These informal observations provide an evidential base for deciding which, if any, children should be exposed to more formal assessment. Much clinical insight is involved in selective screening because during the informal observation phase professionals are actually involved in a process of predicting which children are most likely to encounter future difficulties and therefore are likely to benefit from being exposed to the full screening process.

When staff members are both well trained and experienced, selective screening can be both efficient and effective;

efficient because it reduces the costs associated with mass testing. Unfortunately, there are no validated rules for deciding whether or not a particular staff possesses sufficient expertise to conduct selective screening effectively. One method which has been used to determine whether or not selective screening should be adopted by a school district is "self-evaluation," a method whereby staff members reveal perceptions of their own capabilities, often to an outside consultant. In "self-evaluations," staff members ask of themselves the following kinds of questions:

- Do I believe that persons in my professional role should be expected to make initial identifications of children who are likely to have special needs?

- Do parents ever contact me directly about their childrens' special needs and if so, do I feel able to help them?

- Have I developed opinions about which types of special needs or handicaps should receive the highest priority in CHILD-FIND within my school district?

- Does my job permit me to observe children in sufficient depth to document referrals for diagnostic evaluations?

- Do I feel comfortable in performing screening functions without close supervision?

When staff responses to these kinds of questions are generally positive, chances are good that the staff will support a selective screening program and make it work. But even then, if a large proportion of a staff has fewer than three years' of experience working with children and if some of them have little or no university preparation in the problems and characteristics of handicapped or special needs children, the selective screening option may be a poor choice.

It should be noted that it is always possible to shift from comprehensive to selective screening or vice versa. No school district should remain entrenched in a pattern of special identification activities solely because of tradition or past decisions. A common reason for shifting from one type of screening program to another is that staff turnover dramatically alters the type of screening program that would be best suited for a school sytem.

By observing, evaluating, and participating in many screening programs, the present author has concluded that classroom teachers show tremendous variability in their competence to detect and report signs of learning impediment or special need. Most frequently overlooked by classroom teachers are signs of mild mental retardation, hearing impairment, auditory perception disorder, and poor health. This occurs more often if children of passive temperament and conforming behavior are involved.

Another form of selective screening worth noting occurs when provisions are made for parents to take their children to diagnostic or clinical centers for professional assessment. Children with more severe learning impediments are usually detected when these provisions are available. A correlation tends to exist, however, between use of services and one's education and socio-economic status. That is to say, parents who are better educated and more affluent tend to make greater use of the diagnostic and clinical resources in the community.

Neither providing in-service programs for professionals nor providing "outreach" services to the home to encourage parents to take advantage of community resources can overcome the basic disadvantage of selective screening. There is added risk that awareness of an incipient problem may occur too late to initiate optimum early interventions.

The present author estimates that among those that engage in any form of screening whatsoever, fewer than 25% of the school districts in the United States provide comprehensive screening. This estimate is based on statewide survey data from some of the larger states and direct observation of many screening programs throughout the nation. A trend toward establishing more comprehensive screening is beginning to appear, however. This trend is, in part, a reaction to the new legislation mandating special needs identification activities.

FIXED SCREENING PROCEDURES

A second important policy question that should be resolved while screening programs are in the planning stage is whether the same screening devices will be used with all children. Similarly, will each school or clinical facility within a given area be required to adhere to the same screening procedures? A "fixed" screening policy is one that requires all children in all schools within a certain boundary to be assessed by the same procedures and instruments.

A policy establishing "fixed" screening may be developed at any level: national, state or local. The advisability of fixed screening programs at the state level has been widely debated but remains unresolved in most states.

Those who vigorously support fixed screening policies argue that a coherent data base will result. Information is developed which can be coded in a single format for efficient storage and analysis. Furthermore, when the data base is consistent, meaningful cross-comparisons can be made between schools or geopolitical entities, e.g., counties. Trends can be plotted. Meaningful summary statistics can be compiled to meet federal and state reporting requirements.

A fixed screening policy can also reduce professional confusion and inefficiency because with the passing of time, professional staff persons become more familiar with the screening devices as their skills improve and they are better able to form insights into the conditions that produce particular responses. In the same sense, fixed screening policies over a wide geopolitical area allow for the construction of high quality in-service packages which are applicable to wide audiences. Through these in-service packages, staff skill can be improved even in view of high job mobility by teachers between schools within a state.

Yet despite the many convincing points favoring fixed screening, a major effect remains uncorrected: no single screening device has yet been developed which detects the many learning impediments that appear among children, to the satisfaction of all professionals. One of the reasons for this situation is that there exists an absence of unanimity regarding the nature and types of learning impediments for which evidence can and should be sought through screening.

Another problem is that in order to be comprehensive, a fixed screening procedure would be very long and time consuming in order to provide evidence concerning the many types of special needs. Shortening assessments to one or two items each, targeted to the full array of handicaps or special needs may produce unreliable measures since reliability decreases rapidly when the numbers and items in a test are reduced.

Variable screening, on the other hand, allows each school and sometimes each professional to formulate screening procedures and to select instruments and methods that are believed to be appropriate to the immediate situation. Also, assessments may be changed from one occasion to another, or from one case to another.

A modified version of variable screening is to provide staff persons with a list of approved instruments and procedures from which they are permitted to choose. The devices and procedures listed would have undergone careful study by a general committee representing the school district and would have met or exceeded minimal standards.

LOCALLY DESIGNED INSTRUMENTS

Where variable screening programs exist we sometimes encounter reliance on instruments designed by the same staff persons that use them. Frequently these screening instruments are composed of portions of other instruments, modified according to the user's perception of local needs. In the opinion of the present author, locally designed instruments are inadequate.

A major reason for the inadquacy of locally designed instruments is that school systems, unless they are very large or very affluent, rarely employ staff with sufficient experience in test development and test evaluation to determine the excellence of new instruments. Since screening devices are concerned with developmental phenomena, those constructing them must also have an understanding of human growth and development, both physical and psychological, which exceeds the level that teachers typically acquire in their teacher preparation programs.

To develop screening devices and observation procedures with a high level of excellence, studies must be conducted to determine whether the devices function as they should, and whether they are reliable and valid. Most school districts are unable to support this basic research because it involves following students over much of their school career to determine the accuracy of predictions. These long term development activities conflict with what is usually an immediate need for a screening instrument. When immediate needs take precedence, instrument development stages are deleted or compressed with the result being poor instruments.

Those who favor the use of locally designed instruments claim that by permitting screening devices to be developed at the district level one is better able to take into account local population characteristics, for example, ethnic or economic composition. In posing this argument, professionals are asserting that the technical excellence of the instrument or procedure is of less consequence than its compatability with local conditions. Assuming that this position is defensible, a problem that remains unresolved is that local variations relevant to screening instrument construction have not been clearly identified. Of even greater consequence for instrument development, no principles, rules, or guidelines have been established which would allow test developers to take into account these local variations, other than very obvious ones such as "design screening instruments in Spanish for Spanish speaking children."

Another ill-advised practice is to allow school districts to design their own instruments by picking and choosing items and components from among several tests to assemble a new one containing what is thought to be the "better" or "more acceptable" portions of the originals. This is a poor practice unless reliability and validity analysis is done on the new composite screening instrument. The reason for this is that subtests taken alone, for example "copying" from the *Metropolitan Readiness Test,* have low reliabilities and validities. Subtests rarely, if ever, display adequate reliabilities and validities. Unfortunately, few test manuals caution users against relying on subtest results. The *Metropolitan Readiness Test* is one of the few that contains a warning against assuming that subtest scores are as reliable and valid as the total score.

ASSESSMENT SKILLS

A generalization which applies to screening is: the more objective the scoring procedure, the less training that will be required of the examiner. For instance, the *Peabody Picture Vocabulary* test requires only that a child point to a picture depicting the object or concept named. The examiner provides verbal cues of the form: "Show me ＿＿＿＿＿＿＿."

The response is then recorded and the examiner turns the page, repeating the procedure. Devices of this type require little training to use.

The general trend has been toward adopting screening instruments that can be administered by persons with limited training; volunteers, parents, or paraprofessionals. Therefore, tests that involve little subjectivity and for cost considerations, those that can be administered in group settings are sought. Once a decision has been made to use teachers or paraprofessionals as examiners, however, a number of screening instruments are excluded from adoption because they require special and extensive training to use. (See the Instrument Profiles chapter for information on specific instruments.)

WHEN TO SCREEN

Educational theorists suggest that it is advisable to institute screening programs as early as possible in the life of the child, sometime during the prekindergarten years. The paradox of this is that it is very difficult to find screening instruments that have been shown to be effective with very young children in detecting special needs. Most published tests are unsuitable for this age group. Perhaps the development of good assessment devices for prekindergarten children is a formidable task because of the immaturity and limited repertoire of responses of children of prekindergarten level. There exists only a very narrow range of item types that are suited to this population. To make matters worse, prekindergarten children are noted for producing unstable responses in assessment situations, i.e., their responses change from one session to the next.

If the decision is made to comprehensively screen prekindergarten children, the logistical problems are enormous. When parents are requested to bring their children to central locations for screening, many will fail to do so even if the screening site is just around the corner. Of all children seen in a recent vision and hearing screening program in an urban community in Illinois, only thirty percent were brought by parents. The rest were enrolled in preschool programs of some type. Unfortunately, it is often those who are most in need of early intervention and diagnosis who fail to appear for prekindergarten screening.

"Outreach Programs" which take the screening process into the home are extremely expensive unless a two-stage screening is conducted. In the first stage, parents are asked to respond to a limited number of simple questions concerning their child's physical status and behavior. On the basis of parent responses to these kinds of questions, a selective screening is addressed to those children who appear to be higher risk. But for this approach to be successful, the community must be fully canvassed in the first stage. This process is sometimes termed a "high risk census."

A final problem associated with prekindergarten screening is that a certain number of "misses" will emerge due to instrument unreliabilities and the added fact that some special needs only begin to become detectable after the child has entered more formal school settings, e.g., learning disabilities, school adjustment problems, social problems. A "miss" is a child who has passed initial screening but later displays failure patterns associated with special needs. To minimize "misses," some school systems screen at prekindergarten, kindergarten, and again at first grade and even later. Repeated screenings result in more reliable conclusions but elevate costs well beyond what might be considered reasonable by many schools.

The most common screening pattern in the United States is to conduct fixed screening at kindergarten level and selective screening later. At the kindergarten level a number of published tests become available for application and the normative basis for making comparisons and interpreting performance differences becomes more adequate. Schools that target screening to the kindergarten level child usually schedule screening near the close of the kindergarten year. This is because kindergarten curriculum is designed to enhance readiness skills, and some problems that might be noted in screening earlier in the year disappear as a consequence of the instructional program. However, for those children displaying "high risk" characteristics at the close of the kindergarten year, options for modifying instructions or introducing special corrective procedures are reduced.

Limiting the value of kindergarten screening is the fact that most school districts lack "transitional programs," a type of further readiness experience between kindergarten and first grade. Therefore, children identified as "high risk" in kindergarten screening often move directly into first grade situations with perhaps some limited resource or support services.

Another option is to screen children at grade levels above kindergarten. But once the child has entered into the numerical grade levels, the onset of failure, maladaptation, and other problems is rapid. Early academic failures set the tone for later performance and foster inflexible patterns of poor learning adjustment.

6

Building Community Awareness

Effective early childhood screening for special needs begins in the home. Unfortunately, parents and other members of the community are often uninformed about the importance of early detection of handicapping conditions, uncertain as to the importance of early warning signs, and unaware of the resources available to them through the public schools. Therefore, in building a good screening program our attention should be first directed to finding ways of improving community awareness of special needs and the services that the schools provide.

PARENTS AND SCREENING

In our society, any involvement by parents with the schools is voluntary until their child reaches age six. Community screening programs for preschool children depends upon voluntary compliance, i.e., not only must parents be willing to have their child tested, but also be willing to take the child to some location where this occurs. Even with school age children, most states now require parents' permission prior to their child being examined or tested. Experience shows us that parent cooperation with formal screening programs sponsored by community agencies is better if parents are fully informed about the program's purpose.

Unfortunately, in our society a correlation exists between socio-economic status and being informed, involvement with the schools, and awareness of the early signs of learning impediments. Parents from higher socio-economic classes tend to have more awareness of good child-rearing practices, symptoms of physical and psychological disorders, and are therefore more aggressive in seeking professional assistance when a problem exists. Furthermore, higher socio-economic status parents tend to have more informal involvement with physicians and other professionals, such as teachers and phychologists, with whom they engage in dialogues.

One of the important purposes of a community awareness program is to help remedy the maldistribution of information and resources pertaining to children's special needs. Another reason for seeking parent involvement in early screening is that parents of young children experience many hours of direct observation and interaction with their children. Their extensive direct observation places them in a position of being able to supply more detailed information than any other source. Professionals and parents commonly express surprise when contrasting their observations of the same child; the segments of behavior which are observed by a "strange" professional in a limited session of involvement are often in sharp contrast with those seen by parents.

OBSERVING MORE CLOSELY

Basically, a community awareness program:

1. encourages parents and others to observe young children more closely;

2. tells them what to look for;

3. tells them what to do if they detect a potential problem;

4. helps relieve any fears about revealing problems; and

5. is an "ongoing process."

If you were to pose a general question to most parents as to whether they watch their child's development fairly carefully, their answer would probably be yes. Yet, many parents are unable to provide accurate answers to specific questions such as "How old was your child when he began to play games with other children?" The reason for their imprecision is that while parents may observe their child fairly carefully as he grows, isolated events have limited significance in and of themselves. Parents lack a frame of reference for observing and lack a purpose for zeroing in on particular behaviors or events.

A community awareness program helps parents acquire observation skills by providing them with a reason for observing *particular behaviors.* It tells them some of the important things to look for when observing their children.

KNOWING WHAT TO LOOK FOR

One of the effective procedures used by the Southwest Illinois Regional Special Education Association, for improving parent and community awareness of handicapping conditions, is the wide distribution of a pamphlet for parents called, *Parents: Do You Know the Early Warning Signs of Children with Special Needs?* This was adapted from material assembled by the Consortium of State Departments of Education of the Appalachian Region, Charleston, West Virginia. Their short list of common indications of developmental problems provides parents with a frame of reference; it is short enough to not be overwhelming. Like advertising, community awareness programs go directly to the central point. This goal being to cause parents to contact professionals for more complete evaluation and follow up if there is any evidence of a problem.

> The following *Early Warning Signs* are some of the more common indications that a problem may exist. If for any reason you suspect that your child may have special needs, we urge you to seek help immediately — don't wait until your child enters school before you begin to deal with the problem.

Seeing

- Often unable to locate and pick up small objects within reach.
- Frequently rubs eyes or complains that eyes hurt.
- Has reddened, watering or encrusted eyelids.
- Holds head in a strained or awkward position (tilts head to either side, thrusts head forward or backward) when trying to look at a particular person or object.
- Sometimes or always crosses one or both eyes.

Talking

- Cannot say "Mama" and "Dada" by age 1.
- Cannot say the names of a few toys and people by age 2.
- Cannot repeat common rhymes or TV jingles by age 3.
- Is not talking in short sentences by age 4.
- Is not understood by people outside the family by age 5.

Playing

- Does not play games such as peek-a-boo, patty cake, waving bye-bye by age 1.
- Does not imitate parents doing routine household chores by age 2 or 3.
- Does not enjoy playing alone with toys, pots and pans, sand, etc., by age 3.
- Does not play group games such as hide-and-seek, tag-ball, etc., with other children by age 4.
- Does not share and take turns by age 5.

Thinking

- Does not react to his/her own name when called by age 1.

- Is unable to identify hair, ears, nose and mouth by pointing to them by age 2.

- Does not understand simple stories told or read by age 3.

- Does not give reasonable answers to such questions as "What do you do when you are sleepy?" or "What do you do when you are hungry?" by age 4.

- Does not seem to understand the meaning of the words "today," "tomorrow," and "yesterday" by age 5.

Hearing

- Does not turn to face the source of strange sounds or voices by six months of age.

- Has frequent ear aches or running ears.

- Talks in a very loud or very soft voice.

- Does not respond when you call from another room.

- Turns the same ear toward a sound he/she wishes to hear.

Moving

- Is unable to sit up without support by age 1.

- Cannot walk without help by age 2.

- Does not walk up and down steps by age 3.

- Is unable to balance on one foot for a short time by age 4.

- Cannot throw a ball overhand and catch a large ball bounced to him/her by age 5.

SERVICES PROVIDED

As a part of a community awareness program it is advisable to provide an overview of the services that are offered by the schools for children with special needs. This information helps parents understand how the schools function and emphasizes that "screening" is part of a total educational program. It goes without saying that "screening" is of little value without the availability of intervention programs. What we wish to avoid is the idea that screening is a process of labelling "defective" children. The description of the services that are provided by the schools does not need to be elaborate, but just enough to indicate that follow-up help is available.

The following illustration is from a "press release" circulated in the newspapers and radio stations by the Southwest Illinois Regional Special Education Association. It should be noted that most media provide free space for public service announcements, of which information about handicapping conditions and school services should be an instance.

Southwest Illinois Regional Special Education Association (SIRSEA) provides free supplementary educational services to public schools and private agencies in Jersey, Madison, St. Clair, Monroe, Randolph, and the southern half of Macoupin Counties. SIRSEA serves children with "low prevalence" handicaps, the hearing impaired-deaf, visually impaired-blind, physically handicapped, multiply handicapped, severely emotionally disturbed, and profoundly mentally retarded. The program includes two diagnostic centers, an educational media and information center (REMIS), professional consultants, psychologists, therapists, and a social worker to assist school and private facilities in providing educational services for handicapped children.

SIRSEA emphasis is on the preschool child. It is impossible to overstate the importance of early evaluation and assessment of handicapping conditions. Many children are born with or may acquire physical and/or mental conditions which handicap their normal growth and development. Many of these conditions can be helped or completely corrected if parents recognize the problems early and seek help. The failure to recognize and deal with a problem early may result in an unnecessary life-long handicap.

COMMUNITY CONTACT PERSON

One of the points that should be emphasized in a community awareness program is that there is a particular person within the school system who is charged with the responsibility of following up on requests for evaluations of children or other problems of identifying children with special needs. Assigning responsibility to a particular person is recommended because this tends to personalize and humanize the service offering. Many parents are wholly unfamiliar with the functioning of the school system and are reluctant to initiate contacts with an "impersonal" agency. Also, assigning direct responsibility for community liaison to a staff member is good administrative practice because it focuses responsibility. Public awareness messages should include the community contact person's name, telephone number, hours during which he/she can be reached, and if possible a photograph. Attending to these details enhances the likelihood that parents will initiate contacts when they are troubled by some aspect of their child's development.

The following is an example of a Southwest Illinois Regional Special Education Association public awareness message that includes information about the contact person.

The _____ Public Schools wish to emphasize the importance of locating and identifying preschool handicapped children. To help determine if a problem exists and the severity of the problem, a diagnostic team is available, including audiologist, speech pathologist, diagnostic teacher, and medical consultant. A child may be evaluated by one or more of these persons depending on the need. These services are free to parents. For personal assistance or information, contact:

    _____ (agency)
    _____ (address)
    _____ (telephone number)
    _____ (person's name)
    _____ (hours available)

NEWSPAPER PUBLIC SERVICE ADVERTISEMENTS

Another method of promoting community awareness which has proved effective is newspaper public service advertising. Many newspapers provide free space for public schools or other agencies engaged in public service activities. It is best to talk with the management of your local newspaper concerning this service and find out what kind of copy is required, lead time, and the costs entailed in putting together an attractive layout. The attractive community awareness newspaper advertisement on the following page shows how helpful

Newspaper Public Service Ads - SIRSEA

Free Educational Assistance For Handicapped Children

Give them a chance at a productive future. Handicapped children can have a productive future if you help them at an early age.

Give Them A Chance

Contact SIRSEA — for free assistance. If you know a child who is deaf-hard of hearing, blind-visually impaired, physically impaired, multiply handicapped, mentally retarded or emotionally disturbed, use the coupon below or call—

332-6576

photographs can be. Remember to get written permission from parents before using any photographs of their children in community awareness bulletins.

REFERRAL BY MAIL

Another recommended practice is to place self-addressed, postpaid, referral cards in the hands of physicians, day care center managers, and clergymen. These persons are uniquely situated in terms of having contact with many children and their parents. These professionals are likely to possess information concerning children who are in need or are "at risk" and are therefore a good source of referrals.

Because of the numbers of children that physicians come in contact with during the routine course of their professional lives, it is sometimes impossible for them to initiate telephone contacts or involve themselves in other lengthy and time consuming referral activities. Under these circumstances the referral postcard is ideally suited. The referral card should not demand detailed information. What the school should obtain is simply sufficient information to allow them to initiate some intelligent contact with the family. It is also important that parents or others be aware that someone has initiated a referral for a particular child. Third party referrals must be handled with sensitivity by the schools.

The following is an example of the referral card distributed to physicians, day care center managers, and clergymen.

CHILD REFERRAL CARD

CHILD'S NAME: _____

_____ PARENT/GUARDIAN

AGE: _____

_____(Street)_____

_____(City)_____ (Phone)

Is child now in school? _____ If so where _____

Name of referring person or agency: _____

_____(Street)_____

_____(City)_____ (Phone)

State briefly, why you feel this child needs special educational assistance: _____

_____

_____

PROCEDURAL SAFEGUARDS

In recent years much controversy, litigation, and conflict has surrounded testing and evaluating children. Details of the conflicts are beyond the scope of the present book, but in general schools have been forced to take steps to prevent charges of arbitrariness, unfairness, and ignoring due process being leveled at them in reference to their identification, classification, and placement practices. To protect the rights of parents, children, and to guarantee a fair and just system, many states have adopted school codes which govern and control, in detail, the relationship between parents and the school system. While there are many variations in the specifics of these school codes, most contain certain common elements which relate to the screening process:

1. Parents are entitled to examine and challange any school record relating to their child's background and education.
2. If an evaluation is initiated at the request of a teacher, the parent should have an opportunity to obtain an independent evaluation by someone other than an employee of the school system.
3. Parents should be notified, in writing, before any testing, identification, or evaluation procedure is initiated by the school.
4. Parents should be supplied with a written description of the evaluation procedures that are to be used.
5. Communications with parents should be in their own native language.

6. Parents should give their consent before any evaluation is conducted.

7. A parent is entitled to an impartial hearing regarding their child's appropriate education.

8. If a child's parents are unknown or unavailable, an advocate or surrogate should be assigned to act in his/her behalf and to represent him/her in matters relating to evaluation and testing.

Before initiating a screening program, during the planning stage, school officials should consider what steps will be taken to insure that their screening activities conform with elements of their state school codes and federal regulations.

ACTIVITIES TO BUILD
COMMUNITY AWARENESS AND INVOLVEMENT

Many concrete steps can be taken to build community involvement in child-find, steps which will at the same time promote greater awareness of children's special needs. Dr. William Whiteside of Southern Illinois University, Edwardsville has developed the following list of recommended activities for the Southwest Illinois Regional Special Education Association, for building community awareness and involvement. These recommendations stress the need for obtaining the cooperation of community leaders and concerned citizens in any child-find effort.

1. The school system may host a meeting of concerned leaders representing a cross section of the community who will be able to advise the school system of the various groups within the community who may need special consideration in terms of language, ethnicity, or culture.

2. The school district may consider establishing a permanent local advisory committee for the same purposes as listed above, to advise and assist in the preparation of such materials. Individuals on such a committee may assist and/or recommend others who can assist with the writing of materials in languages other than English.

3. The school system, or either of the above groups, will probably request that a local survey be taken to document the number of persons/families represented in each language/ethnic/cultural group.

A public awareness program, in addition to enlisting the support of families whose children may have special education/developmental problems and needs should inform parents concerning the availability of services, the human rights and legal rights of exceptional children, and what steps to take in order to initiate action on a problem. *The following represent specific public awareness activities which serve, in many instances, a latent screening function.*

1. If the district has a newsletter that is mailed to each parent of a school child in the community, a special issue may be printed to describe the special education program and the rights of handicapped pupils. If the

district has no such newsletter, it may consider creating one for this purpose.

2. The traditional "send a note home with the kids" may be used, but it has not been found to be particularly effective. A signed return slip could be provided to enable the district to mail out such notices to those parents whose children did not return the signed slip.

3. Notices in the form of special interest ads, or in feature articles, may be carried by both metropolitan and local newspapers.

4. Spot announcements on radio and TV or short features on newsworthy programs may be used.

5. During Exceptional Children's Week in the month of May particular effort should be exerted.

6. Special displays created by regional materials centers, by local media people, or by classes may be displayed in local shopping centers.

7. Teachers and other school personnel may volunteer as speakers for various service and social organizations. The local district should make their services known to these groups. Slide presentations would be of assistance.

8. One or more civic/social groups may take on the publication of such services as their special interest project for the year.

9. The district may establish a Special Education Day in the community including such activities as open house, guided tours, teas, etc.

10. The school district may creat a "Special Education Program of the Month" to focus attention on specific services.

11. The local district may create a special award of the month to various persons within the community who have assisted exceptional students and their programs within the public schools.

12. Someone within the community may establish a special education flea market with items for sale that may be used by various types of handicapped children, such as clothing, puzzles, games, walkers, wheelchairs, special chairs, special tables, magnifiers, etc. The local district could also have an information booth and brochures available.

13. The county Advisory Committee may hold meetings, and/or information sessions in various communities in the county.

14. Arts and crafts fair for the handicapped. Exhibits could include the handicrafts of exceptional children, professional personnel working with exceptional children, others interested in exceptional children. Space rental or a percentage of sales could be donated for special equipment or activities for special classes. Again, the district could take advantage of the opportunity for publicity for the dissemination of information.

15. A number of these activities can be used spearately or in combinations at the various local and county homecomings in the community.

Many of the activities that will assist in the location of exceptional children are the same as, or may be combined with, the activities listed under Public Awareness. The following suggestions are those that are specific to the act of locating exceptional children.

1. The school district may convene a meeting of representatives of various state, county, local and/or parents groups concerned with the education and welfare of exceptional individuals. The purpose of such a meeting would be to gather suggestions and perhaps assistance with the location of handicapped individuals between the ages of 3 and 21 residing in the community who may need special educational services. Such a meeting would also avoid duplication of services or prevent gaps in services.

2. Annually, screening may be conducted for exceptional children. Such screening may be conducted via the suggestions made under public awareness. In addition, special contacts and/or information may be provided various medical personnel, private preschools, day care centers, or social agencies most likely to have contact with preschool children.

3. Hearing and vision screening should be conducted at regular intervals. The time of such screenings should be provided parents within the district and an invitation extended to have them bring in other children in the family that they would like to have screened.

4. Speech and language screening should be done upon initial enrollment in the district and at such times as it appears necessary.

5. Annually, all teachers in the district, and other professional personnel, should screen the children with whom they have contact, and make referrals to the appropriate sources.

6. All types of screening may be conducted, on an ongoing basis, to encourage the parents and members of the community having children to look to the local schools as a source of assistance if they suspect that a child may have any type of problem which may interfere with his educational progress either now or in the future.

7

Approaches
to Classification

A quality community awareness program will result in
many referrals, particularly children with low incidence problems such as severe emotional, hearing, visual, physical and
multiple impairments. However, in planning for follow-up
evaluation, or in planning a screening of children already enrolled in school, professionals must proceed from an organizing base, a structure for diagnosis, intervention, professional
communication and management. The present chapter reviews
some generic structures that have provided a basis for classification and some of the important issues pertaining to selecting one. The information is meant to provide planners with a
wider perspective for making decisions about the general organization of a screening program and follow-up services.

OVERCHOICE

Since the late 1950's there has been a continuing growth
in the amount of public funds available to support programs
and services for children who are handicapped and/or display
special needs. Along with this increased expenditure of re-

sources to support the education of children with special needs has occurred an increase in the numbers of new professionals working in special education and related disciplines. In their efforts to provide higher quality services to children with special needs, these new professionals have questioned existing practices and suggested alternatives. Some of the existing practices that have been questioned and the alternatives that have been proposed involve the fundamental organizing structures or classifications around which special education services have been organized.

One of the most important issues raised by professionals in recent years has been, "Who is the child with special needs?" and "How can these needs be best described?" In other words, what should be the basic structural model around which we shape our testing, curriculum, and program organization? It is important to recognize that there is no universally accepted definition of the "special needs child," "handicapped child," or "exceptional child." Even these major concepts are in a continuing state of change and revision. However, it is also important to recognize that the definition of the "exceptional," "handicapped," or "special needs" child that is adopted will in part determine:

1. Estimated incidences.

2. Variety and scope of services provided.

3. Number and kinds of assessments used.

4. Curriculum structure.

5. How you think about and relate to the "special needs" child.

Traditional definitions of "exceptional" or "handicapped" children, rather than describing specific conditions or observable, behavioral characteristics, have tended to be administrative devices that communicate rules or guidelines for determining when and how it would be appropriate to classify a child as "exceptional" within the school. These traditional definitions have often been linked to the "demand structure" of the schools, referring to the performance of a child in a school setting. A criticism of this approach is that the child is defined as "exceptional" in terms of an assumed need for modifying school practices, and therefore concerns only a portion of his/her total behavior. In other words, some definitions assert that a child is "exceptional" when because of difficulties he/she is experiencing, it becomes necessary to modify ineffective school practices. One of the more widely accepted definitions of the "exceptional child" is of this type:

> The exceptional child is defined as the child who deviates from the average or normal child (1) in mental characteristics, (2) in sensory abilities, (3) in neuromuscular or physical characteristics, (4) in social or emotional behavior, (5) in communication abilities, (6) in multiple handicaps to such an extent that he requires a modification of school practices, or special educational services, in order to develop to his maximum capacity. (Kirk, 1972)

Other approaches to the definition of the "exceptional child," the underlying construct in any screening program, have stressed that:

1. A child is neither "normal" nor "exceptional" because a child's performance may be "normal" in one context or situation but "exceptional" in another.

2.   "Exceptional" may refer to only a small set of be-
     haviors such as school adjustment.

3.   If a child has shown evidence of special educational
     needs, it does not necessarily mean that this should
     be considered a permanent "characteristic" or "attri-
     bute."

Dunn's (1973) approach to defining the classification
"exceptional child" takes into account these concerns:

> An exceptional pupil is so labelled only for that segment of
> his school career (1) when his deviating physical or behavior-
> al characteristics are of such a nature as to manifest a signi-
> ficant learning asset or disability for special education pur-
> poses; and, therefore, (2) when, through trial provisions, it
> has been determined that he can make greater all-around
> adjustment and scholastic progress with direct or indirect
> special education services than he could with only a typical
> regular class program.

The two preceding general definitions demonstrate the
discrepancies that exist in even such basic areas as the definition of the entire target population to which screening is addressed. Dunn's definition of the "exceptional child" cautions educators and other professionals who might otherwise
be quick to apply "categorical labels" to children or otherwise "type" them. Dunn's definition also allows for the possibility of inferior curriculum, program organization, testing,
administration, supervision, and instruction as being potential
contributors to children's problems.

Some of the cautions and constraints that are found in
Dunn's (1973) definition arose from the fact that professionals recognized that some of the descriptors of special need

such as "mentally retarded" carried negative and unwanted connotations both among laymen and professionals. As early as 1943 professional concern for this problem was manifest when Rivlin (1943) said that "an inoffensive term" should be used to describe the mentally retarded. But in seeking remedies to these and other problems through defining and redefining the structural basis around which services for the "special needs" child, and the language we use in referring to him/her, some confusion and overchoice has resulted. And from the overchoice and lack of professional consensus has emerged discontinuities among schools in how they approach the identification of special needs.

CATEGORICAL STRUCTURES
AND ASSOCIATED CRITICISMS

Medical, psychiatric, psychological, educational and psychometric criteria have traditionally been used to classify children as special needs, exceptional, or handicapped. From these disciplines have emerged terms such as learning impaired, learning disabled, visually handicapped, visually impaired, speech disordered, speech impaired, psychotic, emotionally disturbed, maladjusted, retarded, sub-average intellectual performance, mentally handicapped, mentally defective, mildly retarded, borderline, multiply impaired, multiply handicapped, and so on. There are many more terms in our expanding professional vocabulary.

A valuable system or taxonomy for bringing order to this semantic disarray was proposed by Stevens (1961). To his logical organizing system three concepts are central: *impairment, disability, and handicap.*

Impairment refers to the organism; it means a basic physical defect of the skeletal, muscular, or organ systems. Asthma is an impairment, a paroxysmal disorder of respiration.

In screening, a number of children will be identified for follow-up evaluations who are likely to ultimately display learning problems or school adjustment problems but who show no impairments; there is no verifiable organismic defect present. These children may be intact according to what all of our present observational and diagnostic procedures disclose.

At the same time that no impairments are evident for a child, a disability may be clear and pronounced. A disability is an observable failure to perform required tasks consistent with some standard. These may be school tasks or performances that are expected and required at home. More often, educators are more interested in disabilities that relate to classroom learning and school adjustment. The Minneapolis Behavior Profile, which is described later in the chapter, provides a list of specific school-related disabilities, e.g. "has trouble discriminating between sounds of letters or words."

The third concept, "handicap," refers to the responses that are made by others to the disability or imprairment. It refers to the social consequences of failure to perform important tasks according to a socially accepted standard. For example, the hearing impaired child whose hearing deficit results in imprecise articulation or voice problems may be received as "funny" or with concerns for "What's wrong with him/her?" In the case of overt physical impairments, such as extreme obesity, the visual aspects of the condition may produce avoidance behaviors by "others" (Fanning, 1974). Actions which are directed toward a child and which tend to result in his/her isolation, differential treatment, and limit his/her life's chances are elements of a handicap. The responses of others to a child's inability to perform expected tasks become an important part of the handicap.

Consistent with the Stevens (1961) approach is a recent "streamlined" version of a categorical structure which draws attention to disabilities (Gardner, 1973). Each of these general disability conditions could serve as a target for screening; for example:

> *Behavioral Disabilities.* These include the emotionally disturbed, socially maladjusted, and juvenile delinquent. Associated with this are "a variety of excessive, chronic, and deviant behaviors ranging from impulsive and aggressive to depressive and withdrawal acts which (1) violate the perceivers expectations of appropriateness, and (2) which the perceiver wishes to see stopped." (Graubard, 1973)

The above example of a "disability" definition represents an attempt at providing a brief description of a child's general problem which communicates something about the nature of the special need and provides a basis for classification. However, there are some professionals who believe that all classification systems should be abandoned and that our educational provisions should be constructed *noncategorically.* Those who adhere to this position would replace even "disability" categories with individual diagnoses that are "deficit specific" or "criterion-referenced." Approaches of this type direct our attention toward exact behavioral descriptions of performance and involve a very detailed analysis of a child's functioning, e.g. "has problems telling how things differ."

Those who advocate replacing "disability" categories with specific, detailed, behavioral statements have argued that all categorical systems are undesirable because they:

1. Label children.
2. Lead to social "stigma."
3. Promote ignoring of differences among children within a category.
4. Promote illusion of exaggerated differences between categories.
5. Produce "self-fulfilling prophecies."
6. Contribute to the social isolation of some children.

When the "medical model" was influential in special education, much effort was directed toward analyzing the *causes* of "disabilities." The influence of the medical model in special education resulted from a historical progression wherein physicians and psychiatrists assumed a leadership role in research and diagnosis. Also, there existed the persistent belief that etiological investigations would result in the discovery of the "causes and cures" of "disabilities." Central to this approach was the idea that if the "impairment" could be identified and understood, some corrective treatment might remove its cause and then development could proceed normally. Exaggerated attention to identifying the "causes of problems" and manipulating them rather than attempting to reshape present and immediate behavior has been very apparent in the education of the emotionally disturbed and the remediation of reading disabilities.

Today, emphasis has generally shifted to specifying with a good deal of accuracy and precision, a child's exact performance. Also, curriculum planning for the special needs child frequently involves a "task analysis" which attempts to break down more global behaviors into molecular units.

CRITERION-REFERENCED TAXONOMIES AS AN ORGANIZING BASE FOR PROGRAMMING

The criterion-referenced approach to analyzing learning and behavior problems has focused more attention on describing a child's performance than on naming the child's condition or searching for its cause. In limiting their concerns to immediate behaviors, professionals have sought to avoid making assumptions such as "academic deficits are caused by mental retardation." They have sought to avoid such speculations because once such a classification had been diagnostically verified, educators still remained unclear as to the best approach to use. Educational treatments were not clearly and directly linked to knowledge of the diagnostic category to which a child was assigned.

A more behavioral or "criterion-referenced" approach to diagnosis recognizes that an educational program does not treat mental retardation. Educational programs for special needs children are designed to remediate adaptive behavior deficits or provide practice using various cognitive skills. Therefore, "criterion-referenced" approaches to classification seek first to determine which specific deficits occur for each individual. Theoretically, remedial interventions can be tied somewhat directly to these diagnostic entities. In this way, diagnosis also provides a basis for curriculum and instructional grouping decisions.

For educators who use the criterion-referenced approach, the problem remains of arriving at some structure for organizing their observations. There are infinite behavioral descriptions that can serve as focal points for diagnosis and instruction. And these behavioral descriptions can be organized in a variety of ways. The tendency, therefore, has been for many different organizing structures and sets of behavioral statements to emerge. No single structure has been wholly accepted by professionals.

For example, in providing a resource service for special needs children, the Minneapolis Public Schools identified 120 "items" which were organized into several areas: 1) concept and language development, 2) auditory perception, 3) visual perception, 4) academic achievement, 5) behavior, 6) interpersonal relationships, 7) physical development. These seven areas illustrate that we can provide a structure for screening and service delivery *without reference to* the child's traditional diagnostic category, e.g. mentally retarded. Each child is dealt with as a unique, individual, case. The following are examples of items used with Minneapolis elementary level children to help determine their special needs. When completed by a teacher or other professional with extensive direct knowledge of the child, they serve a type of screening function:

Yes No

Has trouble making decisions

Remembers only fragments of a series
    of directions

Yes No

Ignores endings of words when reading
Works quickly but inaccurately
Avoids physical contact
Has difficulty copying

In constructing a screening program, decisions should be made regarding the best organizing structure in terms of our present state of understanding and knowledge of classification problems, but these decisions should also reflect available intervention services. If the school's compensatory and remedial programs are already organized along traditional categorical lines, a screening program should be consistent with the existing structure. Screening for deficits which are unrelated to the school's existing or planned intervention programs results in data of limited usefulness. It can be said that the screening program should never be more innovative than the classification system already in place. A "criterion-referenced" screening program would be of little benefit in a district whose services for special needs children are organized along traditional categorical lines.

P. L. 94-142 AND SCREENING

With the enactment of Public Law 94-142, The Education for All Handicapped Children Act, educators may be close to achieving greater consistency and continuity on how they classify special needs. Although they may achieve greater consistency, it does not necessarily follow that the result will be more rational or adequate. But, nevertheless, because of the far-reaching consequences of the legislation, state education agencies have begun to bring their practices into conformity with P. L. 94-142.

Public Law 94-142 specifies a categorical system for service delivery to the handicapped of the nation. A screening program recently instituted in Illinois for non-public school students was organized around categories specified in P. L. 94-142 (indicated by *) and others specified in the Illinois School Code. The following shows the Illinois classification system used for screening and how it compares with the categories specified in P. L. 94-142.

Illinois Screening	P. L. 94-142
Trainable mentally handicpd.	Mentally retarded (*)
Educably mentally handicpd.	Mentally retarded (*)
Physically handicpd.	Orthopedically impaired (*)
Multiply handicpd.	
Learning disabled	Learning disabled (*)
Visually impaired	Visually impaired (*)
Hard-of-hearing	Hard-of-hearing (*)
Deaf	Deaf (*)
Deaf/Blind	
Speech/Language impaired	Speech/Language impaired (*)
Educationally handicpd.	
Behavior disordered	Seriously emotionally disturbed (*)
Other health	Other health (*)

What has occurred is that questions about what is the most viable and parsimonious way of organizing our approach to educating children with special needs has been legislatively resolved. The categories established in P. L. 94-142 may be expected to have a powerful influence on educational practice because they provide the structure for reporting to the federal government on state and local education programs.

8

Evaluating
Instrument Quality

A number of different screening devices are available for educators to select from, some hastily assembled but vigorously promoted. Educators who are selecting instruments to use in screening programs are also experiencing considerable time pressures, attempting to establish procedures prior to Fall, 1978. Given these circumstances, there is a danger that valuable resources will be wasted on screening programs that produce unreliable or uninterpretable data and misinformation. Knowing how to go about evaluating developmental screening instrument quality is therefore a necessary skill for those involved in designing, managing or conducting screening programs.

Few topics have generated more heat and less light than the psychometric qualities of tests as presented in teacher education programs. Too often teachers learn only that instruments should be reliable and valid but are uncertain as to the exact meaning of these concepts. As a consequence for lacking full understanding of the need for technical excellence in any assessment device, instrument quality considerations receive only secondary emphasis in the everyday decision processes that occur in the schools. The purpose of the present chapter is to reexamine the relevance of the reliability and validity concepts in a non-technical language and as they pertain to developmental screening instruments. A number of related quality considerations in evaluating instruments will also be explained.

QUALITY CONSIDERATIONS IN INSTRUMENT SELECTION

Central to the question of instrument quality is the fact that:

1. Poor quality instruments produce uninterpretable data.

2. Uninterpretable data result in erroneous conclusions.

3. Erroneous conclusions result in bad decisions.

4. Bad decisions result in ineffective programming.

5. Ineffective programming entails excess human costs and wasted community resources.

The above sequence of events outlines what may happen when instruments of poor quality are used and emphasizes the negatives. But, unfortunately, a series of reverse relationships does not hold. Good screening instruments do not necessarily lead to effective programming. But without them, poor outcomes are virtually guaranteed. While poor data nearly preclude accurate conclusions, good data do not guarantee that those who view it will do so intelligently.

The central purpose of "screening" is to identify, as early as possible, children who have special needs, children who are likely to be suffering from handicapping conditions already, or who are "at risk" of acquiring one or another disability. Unfortunately, with our current state of the art there is room for major error in this process. No screening instrument has yet been designed that will detect special needs with one hundred percent accuracy.

Two major kinds of errors appear in any screening program involving tests *or* observations, regardless of the program's cost or excellence. The first kind of error causes us to overlook children who are already suffering from disabilities or who later develop them. These are children that our screening methods "miss," they "fall through" the process, only to turn up later after their problems have become more apparent and probably compounded. Often these are children with mild problems or are those whose conditions result from the interaction of school demands and some elusive individual condition, for example, a learning disability. In screening, these errors are referred to as "misses."

At the other extreme, there are children whose performance in screening suggests the presence of a disability or special need but who in reality are quite intact. Sometimes these errors are detected in the secondary diagnostic process and of course this fact supplies another reason why diagnostic follow-up is needed with all children who show evidence of disorder at screening. When provisions are lacking for more intensive and detailed diagnostic follow-up, these same children may become the recipients of expensive and unnecessary special services. Children who at screening appear to have problems but who in fact have none are termed "false positives." Careful evaluation of instrument quality prior to final selection, leads to fewer false positives and misses.

Fortunately, we have achieved an understanding of some of the important test characteristics that produce higher rates of false positives and misses. Therefore, these are the conditions and characteristics that test designers attempt to control. As was mentioned previously, educators should concentrate their efforts on locating higher quality existing instruments rather than trying to construct them, unless they possess high levels of expertise and plentiful resources.

What kinds of things are responsible for the kinds of test inaccuracies that produce false positives and misses? The following are some of the more important ones.

Narrow Samples of Behavior

Short tests reduce staff time and student time costs but provide us with less information. The more we reduce the amount of information that is contained in a test score, the less sure we can be that the performance we see is truly representative of the child's condition or abilities. Short tests involve the assumption that the narrow sample of behavior they are eliciting is "typical" of the child's general performance.

Children's Responses Are Unstable

Many factors influence a child's performance and cause it to be unstable over a very short period of time. The younger the child, the more unstable his performance in an assessment situation. Fatigue, stress, shyness, hostility toward the examiner, and the events just prior to testing the child often influence the child's response to assessment. Typically, tests are sensitive to a wider range of events and conditions than just the behaviors or abilities that the test is designed to detect. These unwanted factors produce individual differences in test performance, but they are unrelated to what the test is designed to assess.

Examiners Influence Outcomes

Since testing is a situation involving human interactions, the relationship that prevails between the child and the examiner influences positively or negatively his performance. If this were equally true for every child and each examiner, we would have fewer problems. But all examiners are different and all children are different. The examiner's unique influence on the child's performance is another unwanted factor that can produce individual differences in performance unrelated to what the test is supposed to be measuring. The more involvement required of the examiner, when he or she actually becomes part of the instrument (as in informal observation), the greater the chance of the examiner influencing outcomes.

Imperfect Administration Instructions

Tests vary in the details that are provided regarding how the test should be administered. How should children be seated? What space, light conditions and sound control is required? What should the examiner say? Tests whose directions provide insufficient details concerning how the test is to be administered and allow different examiners to answer questions like the above, allow differences in student response to emerge that are unrelated to the purposes of the test.

Linguistic and Cultural Biases

Much controversy and litigation has arisen over the use of tests that are "inappropriate" for the target population. What this usually means is that tests are sometimes used which contain content that is not fully understood by the child because he has had a different set of experiences or because he speaks a different language or dialect. If, for example, we are screening for mental retardation and a test with linguistic and cultural biases is used, a number of false positives are generated because we are measuring individual differences in language and cultural experience at the same time we are attempting to measure differences in mental abilities. Therefore, some of the differences we see become spurious or at least uninterpretable.

The five factors explained above are the more important sources of instrument "unreliability." An unreliable instrument discloses individual differences which are unrelated to the overriding purpose of the assessment. When one begins to interpret these differences, or draw conclusions from them, one is practicing the art of interpreting test error, hardly a worthwhile enterprise.

VALIDITY OF DEVELOPMENTAL
SCREENING INSTRUMENTS

To determine a developmental screening instrument's validity over a period of time, one must study the usefulness of the instrument in the context of its ascribed purposes. Ascertaining the validity of a developmental screening instrument is difficult and costly. There are few examples of screening instruments on which sufficient validity studies have been conducted.

When one administers a developmental screening instrument and uses the test results to single out a child for followup, one is actually engaged in prediction. It is being predicted that the child who "passes" the screening test will not develop serious problems in the future and the child who fails *will* develop serious problems. Actually, educators have learned to "hedge" by asserting that the child will "probably" or "may" develop problems. Nevertheless, when test evidence is used as a basis for initiating follow-up diagnosis or intervention the course of action has been selected because it is believed that the child will benefit. There is some degree of trust placed in the data revealed by the assessment.

But the only way to determine whether or not our test-based predictions are accurate is to test young children with developmental screening instruments, store the results, and *not* intervene in any way. Then, in a few years, one seeks evidence of problems in learning and adjustment that may have appeared subsequent to testing. If children who "failed" the assessment all developed learning and adjustment problems it would be clear evidence of the instrument's high "predictive validity."

Few studies of this type have ever been conducted on screening instruments for two main reasons:

1. Sound predictive validity studies involve denying treatment to children who are suspected of needing it, a practice considered unethical.

2. The immeidate need for instruments precludes long-term studies prior to instrument dissemination.

Lacking means to conduct tight predictive validity analysis of screening instruments, test constructors have turned to studies involving "congruent validity." Studying the "congruent validity" of an instrument involves checking to see how consistent the screening test's results are with other, more traditional, detailed, well-established, or individual tests. Two tests commonly used in studies of "congruent validity" as a criterion are the WISC and Stanford-Binet. These are tests on which extensive validity studies have been assembled, and are tests of known properties. If the results obtained from using a particular developmental screening instrument are consistent with results obtained on the same children using "established" tests, the instrument is considered to have shown evidence of "congruent validity." Most validity studies of developmental screening instruments are of this type.

Congruent validity studies tend to produce validity coefficients which are artificially reduced or lowered because of the fact that the test against which the screening results are compared is not wholly free of measurement error (is not perfectly reliable). The maximum congruent validity of a test is equal to the square root of the product of the reliabilities of the two tests that are being compared.

Most often "face" or "consensual" validity is reported for a developmental screening instrument. To establish an instrument's "face" or "consensual" validity several authorities must agree that the instrument assesses what the test designer claims it assesses.

An instrument's reliability is always our first object of technical concern because reliability limits validity in a lawful fashion. A test which is unreliable cannot be valid. Yet a test which is highly reliable is not necessarily valid. The exact nature of the relationship between reliability and validity is the *maximum* validity of a test is equal to the square root of its reliability. If a test's reliability is .81, its maximum validity is .90 when the criterion is free of measurement error. When the criterion, such as another test in the study of congruent validity, is not wholly free of error, the maximum potential validity coefficient is further reduced.

Fortunately, there are several convenient sources of information concerning the technical excellence of screening instruments. These should always be consulted prior to using an instrument. Contained in these sources are the evaluations of experts and specialists who are willing to provide detailed technical criticisms of instruments.

If a particular instrument has not been reviewed in any of the standard sources it does not necessarily mean that the instrument is inadequate or superficial. It is possible that the instrument may have been recently published or have received narrow dissemination. In the event that information on a particular screening instrument cannot be located in standard sources, one should carefully examine the test's technical manual. Perhaps the aid of a special consultant can be enlisted in this effort.

The absolute unavailability of data on a test's technical excellence is a sufficient reason to exclude it from consideration as a part of a screening battery. Tests lacking reliability and validity data may have been hastily assembled for purposes of achieving quick profits. Conducting basic reliability and validity studies on an instrument is not an overwhelming task and the absence of such data usually occurs by design rather than because of a test maker's inability to gather sufficient resources to do the job.

The following is a list of technical references which should be consulted prior to making a final decision concerning the adoption of a particular developmental screening instrument.

1. Buros, O. K. (Ed.). *The Fifth Mental Measurement Yearbook.* Highland Park, NJ: Gryphon, 1959.

2. Buros, O. K. (Ed.). *The Sixth Mental Measurement Yearbook.* Highland Park, NJ: Gryphon, 1965.

3. Buros, O. K. (Ed.). *The Seventh Mental Measurement Yearbook.* Highland Park, NY: Gryphon, 1972.

4. Buros, O. K. (Ed.). *Reading Tests and Reviews.* Highland Park, NJ: Gryphon, 1968.

5. Educational Testing Service. *Test Collection.* Princeton, NJ: Educational Testing Service, 1971.

6. Frakenburg, W. K. & Camp, B. W. (Eds.). *Pediatric Screening Tests.* Springfield, Illinois: Charles C. Thomas, 1975.

7. Hoepfner, R., Stern, C. & Nummedal, S. (Eds.). *CSE-ECRC Preschool/Kindergarten Test Evaluations.* Los Angeles: UCLA Graduate School of Education, 1973.

8. Technical Assistance Development System. *Evaluation Bibliography: Tadscript No. 2.* Chapel Hill, NC: University of North Carolina, 1973.

CSE-ECRC TEST EVALUATIONS

A particularly valuable resource for professionals wishing to obtain general ratings of the technical adequacy of a particular instrument is the *CSE-ECRC Preschool/Kindergarten Test Evaluations.* This resource is a "compendium of tests, keyed to educational objectives of early education, and evaluated by measurement experts and educators for such characteristics as meaningfulness, examinee appropriateness, administrative usability, and quality of standardization. The "periodic table" of tests and objectives is designed for use by school principals and directors who do not necessarily have technical expertise in educational measurement and evaluation, yet its rigorous treatment will make it of interest to educational evaluators and psychometricians."

CSE-ECRC test evaluations are made using the MEAN system, an acronym for:

Measurement Validity

Examinee Appropriateness

Administrative Usability

Normed Technical Excellence

In preparing the CSE-ECRC test evaluations expert reviewers provided numerical ratings for tests according to their interpretation of the test's adequacy using all available data. "Within each of the four evaluative categories (listed above), a letter grade, based on the points assigned to each aspect of each criterion was computed." Tests were rated as good, fair, or poor for each of the MEAN categories. A total grade for each instrument is available. For example, the *Valett Developmental Survey of Basic Learning Abilities* is rated "FGPP," fair in measurement validity, good in examinee appropriateness, poor in both administrative usability and normed technical excellence.

The CSE-ECRC test evaluations are available for 139 instruments at the preschool/kindergarten levels. Only a portion of these tests are developmental screening instruments. While subtests are separately rated, little descriptive information regarding the test as a whole and its intended use is provided. Tests are, however, keyed to curriculum and instruction areas based on a taxonomy of educational objectives.

The writer recommends that CSE-ECRC test evaluations be consulted after using the "Instrument Profiles" contained in the present volume and before or concurrent with consulting standard technical references such as Buros' *Mental Measurement Yearbook* for more detailed discussions of instruments. Ideally, at all planning sessions relating to screening, these reference works would be made available for staff use.

SPANISH VERSION

Despite the large number of Latino children enrolled in the public schools, few tests have been modified for administration in Spanish. To modify a test for use with Latino children is not simply a matter of translating the test, although this approach is better than nothing. Often a test's characteristics change when translation into another language is made. Therefore, it becomes necessary to establish new reliability and validity indices and to also establish separate norms for the new population (Simon and Joiner, 1976).

Although there has been much debate over culturally and linguistically biased assessment devices, there has been little evidence of major new instruments which have surmounted these problems. Some preference should be given, however, to screening tests which have a Spanish version if your school system enrolls Spanish speaking students.

INSTRUMENT'S RANGE

In some instances, school systems wish to organize comprehensive screening programs for children of all ages and all grade levels. A major criteria for instrument selection in this case is the range of ages the instrument is suitable for use with. Instruments that have wider ranges and are therefore appropriate for use at several developmental levels should be sought. Efficiency is increased when variations in the number and types of screening instruments used is kept to a minimum. When different screening instruments with narrow ranges are used at different age levels, interpretation of test results becomes more complex and we are never certain that we have achieved equivalent criteria when shifting from one instrument to the next at different developmental levels.

EASE OF SCORING

Better screening devices generate objective data which can be objectively scored, rated, or interpreted. Little economy is achieved if an instrument is selected on the basis of requiring little administration time, or being simple to administer, if complicated or subjective scoring procedures are involved. Complicated and subjective scoring results in data that is incomparable from examiner to examiner. Each person brings a slightly different orientation to the interpretation task.

A more desirable test will allow for scoring while the test is being administered so that only some form of summation is required at a later date. Generally check lists and rating scales are of this type as are tests such as the *Peabody Picture Vocabulary Test*. Simultaneous administration and scoring makes better use of staff time and since it is more efficient, tests that are easy to score are likely to be met with more enthusiasm by teachers and others responsible for data collection.

INSERVICE TRAINING PROVISIONS

No screening instrument functions automatically; each requires the involvement of someone who either administers an item, structures a task or records a behavioral event. Because of the human involvement in the screening process, variations in results can be produced when examiners bring differing levels of experience and competence to the screening situation. Even tests that are designed for administration by parents or paraprofessionals are sensitive to the "examiner effect."

Because of the "examiner effect" nearly all screening procedures require that examiners receive some training in test administration, observation, and score recording. Examiners must also be aware of standards or success and failure so they can identify students who need to be referred for more detailed diagnosis. Most screening tests entail some subjective judgments by examiners and if young children are involved, as would be desired, examiners must be sensitive to conditions which might impede students in performing adequately. For instance, management problems associated with the structure of the screening situation can produce noise, confusion, and disruption. The presence of these problems tends to invalidate screening results.

The best method for insuring that you are receiving the most accurate information that can be elicited by the instrument is to require that every person who will be associated with the screening process receive some form of inservice education relating to screening. At the minimum, inservice preparation for screening will guarantee that there is a basic continuity in how the data is collected.

TIME AND EXPENSE FACTORS

Evaluating tests for use in a screening program involves an awareness of the need for budgeting several important cost factors:

1. Staff Time
   a. Training
   b. Test administration
   c. Scoring and recording
2. Student Time
3. Test Acquisition and Distribution Costs
4. Second Level Screening and Diagnostic Follow-Up for High Risk Children

It is advisable to establish guidelines or ceilings relating to staff time, student time, test acquisition, and distribution costs. By doing this the school district will immediately rule out some tests or combinations of tests and therefore simplify the test evaluation problem. It should be recognized that the instruments that are selected will determine, to a major extent, the costs associated with the first three items (above).

There are no universal rules that can be applied for deciding how much staff time should be allocated for screening activities, except for the obvious: low costs should be sought. In the opinion of the present author, any educational activity which involves anything other than direct student service, i.e., teaching and counseling, must be considered a cost factor for our educational systems. This does not mean that these activities are unnecessary. A businessman incurs costs in doing business, for example his insurance. He attempts to keep these costs within reasonable bounds, however. Similarly there are many costs related to providing instruction and counseling to students that are necessary but should be kept as low as possible.

The training costs associated with a screening program will vary according to: the complexity of the screening devices chosen for use; the present levels of skills and experience of the staff; the salary levels of persons directly responsible for the screening activities.

At the highest cost level, some school districts have chosen to use instruments for screening purposes which must be administered by school psychologists or diagnosticians. These instruments are actually diagnostic instruments. They are complex and their costs are high in terms of per hour dollar costs for highly paid professionals.

It is recommended, however, that schools adopt screening instruments that can be administered by paraprofessionals who receive inservice training and professional supervision. Generally, tests that are designed for use by teachers can be administered by paraprofessionals if they are provided with supervision and inservice training. Therefore, the present author recommends that one of the first questions to be asked concerning a screening instrument is: "Can it be administered by teachers or does it require an examiner with more extensive training in testing procedures *or content?*"

One area in which it would be questionable to rely on paraprofessionals or teachers as examiners is *speech.* It has been found that teachers are generally lacking in the skills necessary to detect speech and language impairments. Using teacher-examiners for speech screening becomes inefficient because of the need for repeated testing for false positives and misses. A professionally trained speech and language therapist will be able to conduct screening at the rate of about five minutes per child.

An inservice program prior to initiating a screening program should be addressed to:

1. The purpose of the screening program.

2. The time frame during which screening will occur.

3. Examining the instruments that will be used.

4. Using the instruments on a trial and practice basis.

5. A review of the data format . . . how the data is to be recorded.

6. What to do about students that are absent.

7. Where the results are sent and what happens next.

By providing inservice training relating to the above topics it can be assured that teachers will be fully informed and likely to do a better job of screening.

STANDARDS OF EXCELLENCE APPLY TO "SURVEYS"

When an instrument is termed a "survey" is the application of rigorous standards of excellence evaded? Sometimes it is mistakenly concluded that questions of technical excellence are only relevant to "tests." Yet when survey instruments are used as part of a screening program, pupils are ranked, evaluated, classified, or described in terms of the data. Professional actions stem, at least in part, from the data.

When children are ranked, evaluated, classified, or described the resulting generalizations may range from very accurate to very inaccurate. Accuracy involves reliability (the relative amount of error present in a score or ranking) and validity (the extent to which the instrument is eliciting data relevant to our decision process). And when assessments are used for the purpose of making decisions which might alter a child's life's chances or lead to stigmatization of any sort it is reasonable to expect that educators and other professionals take every precaution that instrument error be minimized. At the very least, the level of error for an instrument should be known.

In the writer's opinion, using an instrument of unknown technical excellence at any point in the decision processes of mental health or educational agencies is to be avoided, regardless of whether the instrument is called a "scale," "test," "survey," "instrument," or "assessment device."

AN ILLUSTRATIVE
INSTRUMENT EVALUATION FORMAT

The data shown in Table I illustrate and summarize the results of one review of published tests which were proposed as possible screening instruments for use in a school system (Joiner, 1977). An instrument was proposed that appeared to be a diagnostic instrument, so the first question that was raised was whether each instrument was suitable for use as a screening device. The answer to that question is contained in the column at the far right of Table I. Actually, once it has been

TABLE I: Illustrative Test Review Format Used by Education Agency: Multiple Standards

Columns LD through Prv Acd fall under the heading "Possibly Suitable for Detecting."

Test Name	LD	MR	BD	ED	CD	GB	SMI	Lat Dir	V/A Per	Con Skl	Lan Dev	Prv Acd	Teacher Adm	Pre-Kndgtn	Kindergarten	Grade 1+	Group Test	Spanish Ver	Buros Relia	Buros Valid	Rated "fair" or better in %	UCLA criteria	Screening Instr
A. Tests unsuited for screening																							
1. Illinois T of Psych/linguists	+								+	+	+		?	+	+	+			F	P	N	N	N
B. Tests suited for screening																							
2. ABC Inventory	+						+			+	+		+	+	+	+	+		P	P	N	Y	Y
3. Bender-Gestalt Test	+		+	+	+		+		+V	?	?		+	+	+	+	?		P	P	N	N	N
4. Boehm T of Basic Cncpts	+	+			+		+			+	+		+	+	+	+	+		G	F	Y	Y	Y
5. Coop Preschl Inventory		+			+		+			+	+		+	+	+	+		+	P	G	N	Y	Y
6. Denver Dvlp Screening T	+	+	+	+			+			+			+	+	+	+			G	F	U	Y	Y
7. Dvlp T of Vis-Mot-Integra	?		?				+		+V				+		+	+	+		F	P	Y	Y	Y
8. Dvlp T of Visual Percp							+		+V				?		+	+	+		F	P	N	Y	Y
9. First Grade Screening T		+	+	+			+	+	+AV	+	+		+	+	+	+	+		?	F	U	Y	Y
10. Human Figure Drawing		+	+	+			+						+		+	+	+		F	F	N	Y	Y
11. Meeting Street	+						+		+V		+		+	+	+	+			P	P	U	Y	Y
12. Metropolitan Readiness	+	+					+		+V		+		+		+		+		G	G	Y	Y	Y
13. Peabody Picture Vocab T		+					+						+	+	+	+		+	F	F	Y	Y	Y
14. Percp Forms T (Wntrhvn)	?				?				+V		+		+			+	+		P	P	U	Y	Y
15. Purdue Percp Motor Srvy			+	+									?						?	?			
16. Riley Preschl Dvlp Scrn T		+					+						+	+	+				P	P	U	U	Y
17. Scrn T: Iden Chldn w/ SLD	+						+		+AV				?	+	+	+	+		?	?	U	U	Y
18. Wepman Aud Discrm T	+								+A				+		+	+			F	F	Y	Y	Y

G = Good; F = Fair; P = Poor; U = Unrated; Y = Yes; N = No concluded that an instrument is more suitable for diagnostic applications than for screening, no further examination of its characteristics is necessary.

Under the heading "possibly suitable for detecting" appear abbreviations for the "disability categories" that had been adopted as a classification system for screening. The abbreviations represent:

LD = Learning Disabled
MR = Mentally Retarded
BD = Behavior Disorder
ED = Emotionally Disturbed
CD = Culturally Different
GB = General Behavior
SMI = Sensory-Motor Integration
VA Per. = Visual and Auditory Perception
Con. Skl. = Conceptual Skills
Lan. Dev. = Language Development

Suitability of an instrument for detecting any or all of these conditions was judged by reviewing the items, manuals, technical sources, articles, and reports from users. A plus (+) indicates that the test is probably suitable for detecting evidence of the condition or disability. It does not mean, however, that the test was specifically designed to detect the condition in question. There only seems to be evidence that supports believing that the test could indicate the presence of a condition if interpreted accurately.

Since is was judged desirable or even necessary to use instruments that could be administered by teachers rather than just school psychologists or diagnosticians, an evaluation of each instrument was also conducted on that dimension. Other instrument characteristics that were judged desirable and for which each instrument was rated were:

1. Suitability for use at pre-kindergarten level.
2. Suitability for group administration.
3. Availability of a Spanish version.

Discussions of the instrument in Buros' *Mental Measurement Yearbook* were summarized as generally good, fair, or poor. These generalizations were not relied on heavily because Buors' technical evaluations are usually detailed and rarely contain unequivocal endorsements or condemnations of instruments.

The judging criteria used for instruments rated by CSE-ECRC is more objective than the summaries of the Buros evaluations: "rated fair or better on three of four MEAN criteria."

A similar test review format can be constructed for any group of tests that might be considered by a school staff for a screening program. Different evaluative criteria (the columns in Table I) will probably be used because each school system has different characteristics, resources, and needs. Also, the classifications that are to be used in targeting screening are likely to differ (see Chapter 4).

9

Children's Drawings as Developmental Indices

Developmental assessments involving human figure drawings (HFD) have a long history of use by educators, dating back to at least the 1930's. If one were to examine a random sample of student "cumulative folders" it is likely that a human figure drawing assessment or a test involving one would be more frequently encountered than any other single type of assessment. Responses to one statewide survey indicated that human figure drawings were used to identify every type of "special need" or "handicap," including: learning disabilities, mental retardation, brain damage, emotional disturbance, cultural disadvantage, general behavior, sensory-motor integration, laterality/directionality, visual and auditory perception, conceptual skills, language development, and previous academic achievement (Joiner, 1977). Human figure drawings were identified as the second most frequently used symptomatic criteria next to the *Metropolitan Readiness* which also includes an "optional" figure drawing task. Because of their widespread use and acceptance by educators as screening devices, the present chapter is devoted to a review and discussion of their appropriate application.

TWO USES OF HUMAN FIGURE DRAWING TESTS

Despite the fact that human figure drawing tests are used to assess a variety of special needs and handicapping conditions, not all such applications of these measures can be justified. The two major uses of human figure drawing tests that have been most carefully studied are first, as measures of mental maturity and developmental level and second, as projective personality assessments. Probably the most widely used human figure drawing test for assessing mental maturity and developmental level is the *Draw-A-Man Test* (Goodenough, 1926; Goodenough and Harris, 1963). In the area of personality assessment through projective means, the *Draw-A-Person* (Machover, 1949) has achieved a position of central importance.

More recently, procedures have been developed for scoring results of children's human figure drawings objectively, both for personality and developmental assessment. The more objective procedures were designed for use with data from children ages five to twelve. Koppitz (1968) developed these procedures for scoring, the entire system for objective scoring of human figure drawings being the *Human Figure Drawing Test.*

Since the beginning of systematic attempts to study the usefulness of human figure drawings as a measurement device late in the 19th Century, there has been an "inexorable though slow increase in the consensual and empirical validity of projective drawings" (Ogden, 1976). Ogden, a recognized authority on psychodiagnostics, reported that many studies conclude: human figure drawings are sufficiently reliable for behavioral predictions. But there remain many unresolved problems relating to their use as reliable and valid assessment tools.

CONDITIONS INFLUENCING PERFORMANCE
ON HFD TESTS

While much of the research that has been reported on HFD tests suggests that they possess fair levels of reliability and validity (Guinan and Hurley, 1965; Landsman and Dillard, 1967), it is important to be aware that children's drawings of the human figure vary in quality and content because of a number of conditions and events extraneous to the ascribed purpose of the test. For example, an important source of variation in the quality and detail of figure drawings results from differences among children in *motivation,* a consideration which especially confuses the interpretation of test-retest differences (Schubert, 1969).

Quality and details in drawings of human figures are also influenced by the *level of sensory-motor maturation* of the child performaing the drawing task (Whitmyre, 1953). It is because of their sensitivity to sensory-motor maturation factors, that educators have sometimes used HFD test results as indices of learning disabilities. But while sensory-motor deficits are *sometimes* linked to "learning disabilities," many children of pre-kindergarten and kindergarten level simply lack sufficient sensory-motor readiness to allow them to perform the precision fine motor coordinations required by the human figure drawing task. It therefore becomes impossible, on the basis of this evidence alone, to distinguish between children who are mentally retarded, slow in maturation, and those who are beginning to show the discrepancy between potential and achievement which underlies the concept of "learning disability." Applications of human figure drawings tests as screening devices for "learning disabilities" are therefore questionable.

ARE HUMAN FIGURE DRAWING TESTS
CULTURE FAIR?

Educators have sometimes adopted the use of human figure drawing tests under the mistaken assumption that lacking linguistic content they are "culture fair." Clinicians who use these tests regularly, however, observe that children include elements in their drawings with greater frequency if they have acquired words to conceptualize these elements. Also, there is evidence that culture influences perceptions and that the social experiences of children are reflected in elements children select for emphasis in their human figure drawing (Machover, 1943). Therefore, it can be argued that scoring systems which are based on narrow samples, including only small numbers of children who are culturally different, may lead to inaccurate conclusion concerning the presence or absence of deficits among minority children. The extent to which socio-cultural biases prevail in the scoring of human figure drawing tests has been minimally researched.

CAUTIONS REGARDING SCORING

Although educators have used human figure drawings primarily as evidence of developmental differences and mental maturity, psychologists use these assessments as evidence concerning the existence of personality traits. While an extensive research literature exists on these applications, there is as yet no *fully* adequate objective scoring system for HFD (Buros, 1972). Interpreting and scoring human figure drawings for diagnosis of personality structure can only be accomplished by clinicians with extensive education and experience. Teachers generally lack this capability. However, teachers can use the Koppitz (1968) scoring system for the *Human Figure Drawing Test* to derive a gross index of adjustment suitable for screening purposes. But even under the most carefully controlled circumstances, conclusions regarding the structure of personality or the quality of emotional life derived from an analysis of HFD's are subjective and dependent upon the skills, orientations, and possible biases of the scorer.

It is noteworthy that typically when HFD assessments are mentioned as a means of assessing personality or developmental level, a warning is issued that these indicators should only be considered part of a larger array of data. When used alone for diagnostic or classification purposes human figure drawing tests are misused. Taken alone, they are insufficient evidence to validate a diagnostic conclusion.

MENTAL MATURITY ASSESSMENT

For assessing mental maturity an objective scoring system has been devised for the *Draw-A-Man Test,* (Goodenough and Harris, 1963). Scoring a test requires about ten minutes of a teacher's time. Of course, it is assumed that the teacher has received instruction in the scoring system and has had an opportunity to score samples of student performance under supervised conditions. The interrater reliability of the *Draw-A-Man* scoring system is considered adequate for a gross screening, but the results produced by an individual child may be distorted by situational factors such as interest in the task, conditions under which the test is given, rapport with the examiner, fatigue, and perceived reinforcers. Perhaps as a consequence of these contaminations, a wide range of reliabilities has been reported, from approximately .20 to .70 (Buros, 1972).

Research involving the use of human figure drawings as an index of general intelligence reveals that the strongest relationship occurs between these variables at ages six and seven. By age eleven, the consistency between these measures begin to fade. During adolescence, drawing tasks become poor indices of intellectual functioning because of changes in social roles. For older children, drawing skill becomes less salient. Sex differences begin to consistently appear, males exerting less effort in the production of adequate drawings (Hornowski, 1970).

RECOMMENDATIONS FOR SCREENING

1. Human figure drawings can provide cost-efficient screening for five and six year olds if they are properly administered and scored and if their use is limited to those with established validity. The fact that these measures have achieved wide popularity suggests that educators are convinced that they yield useful information. Their wide acceptance among educators argues for their retention in a screening battery if they are used under controlled conditions.

2. A danger to be aware of is that because scoring systems differ, it is likely that different HFD tests will result in different conclusions regarding an individual child.

3. If a single HFD procedure were sought, the Koppitz "Human Figure Drawing Test" would provide an acceptable option because: 1) it has received fairly wide application and acceptance; 2) it can be administered and objectively scored by teachers; and 3) it yields evidence on both intellectual and emotional factors.

4. Teachers involved in screening should receive in-service instruction on administering and scoring whatever test is selected. It is unlikely that teachers will have acquired sufficient skill in the use of human figure drawing tests in their teacher preparation programs to enable them to apply the tests successfully in screening programs.

5. Even though HFD tests contain no major linguistic elements, teachers must be sensitive to the possibility that socio-cultural factors may influence test outcomes. Evidence regarding the presence of socio-cultural biases in these tests is limited and equivocal.

6. Under no conditions should evidence from human figure drawing tests alone be used for purposes of differential diagnosis or placement. These tests must be used in combination with more detailed diagnostic testing to reveal the actual nature of the child's deficits.

7. The fact that human figure drawing tests lack linguistic and auditory components makes them unsuitable for use as the sole screening instrument for special needs assessment. Overwhelming evidence pertaining to the structure of human abilities indicates that children who

successfully pass screening with HFD tests may experience educational difficulties due to language impairments, auditory perception problems, and inability to deal with conceptual material among other things.

8. Several commonly used screening instruments involve human figure drawings or other drawing tasks, as part of a wider assessment. Included among them are:

Metropolitan Readiness Test

Vane Kindergarten Test

ABC Inventory

Gesell Developmental Schedules

Denver Developmental Screening Test

First Grade Screening Test

Riley Preschool Development Inventory

10
Instrument Profiles*

Professionals who are responsible for planning and implementing developmental screening programs are expected to select instruments that are not only suited to their local needs but instruments that are also rationally defensible. Professionals are legitimately accountable for their instrument selection decisions in the same sense that they are accountable for the implementation and success of their follow-up programs. In order to make the best possible selection of a developmental screening instrument, it is necessary to be aware of the many instruments that are available for consideration. The present chapter serves as an aid to instrument selection by identifying 137 different instruments that might be considered by those planning a developmental screening program. An indication of the presence of selected "desirable" features is provided along with an indication of the type of "special need" assessed by the instrument.

Although the 137 instrument profiles in this chapter provide a broad representation of available developmental screening instruments, new instruments are continuously being developed. Therefore, the listing of profiles cannot be

*For a more detailed, technical discussion of developmental screening tests, see the Bibliography: Davidson, et al., 1977, and L. M. Joiner, 1977.

considered absolutely comprehensive. Readers may be aware of other tests that have recently become available or are in the development stage. It may be worthwhile to review those tests in terms of the parameters suggested in the present chapter.

HOW TO USE THE INSTRUMENT PROFILES

The instrument profiles are meant to serve an initial function of reducing the number of instruments that professionals should review in detail or examine directly when reaching a final decision regarding instruments that will be adopted for use in a developmental screening program. By using the instrument profiles, the program developer may be able to exclude from further consideration a number of instruments which fail to possess certain desirable features which are important in the local context.

It is suggested that the "desirable features" be reviewed and discussed by the committee, individual, or group responsible for planning a screening program. These "desirable features" can be rated as "absolutely necessary," "important but not necessary" and "low importance" according to the intended local application.

Similarly, the special needs that are being targeted for screening may vary from one context to another. In the opinion of the present author, there is no single instrument that will be universally suited to detecting all of the special needs that are of educational relevance. The broader the array of special needs that is targeted for screening, the larger the number of instruments that must be applied in a screening program.

After the instrument profiles have been reviewed, the number of instruments that will require detailed review by program developers will be considerably reduced. After the preliminary review of the instrument profiles it is recommended that the remaining instruments be reviewed in detail using the technical sources identified in Chapter 5, according to the criteria discussed in that chapter. The technical reviews will be very revealing and will tend to further reduce the number of instruments warranting consideration.

Those instruments that remain "in the running" should then be obtained and examined in detail. The technical manuals should be read; if necessary, a technical consultant should be employed to assist in the process of test review. As a final step, trial administrations should be arranged to detect any special problems that might surface during application.

It is also important to remember that parents may wish to participate in the final selection of instruments because they bring to the situation a different perspective and because they are entitled to be aware of just what procedures are being used to identify children with special needs. By undertaking these steps in a systematic way, the schools can decrease the likelihood of controversies arising from the screening program and promote full community cooperation in the effort to identify children's special needs.

INSTRUMENT, ITEM CONTENT AND AGE RANGE

The first item in the instrument profiles provides the prospective user with the name of the instrument, the chronological age (CA) range for which the instrument is claimed to be suited, and the kinds of tasks that are performed in response to the items. One of the criteria that might be used when reviewing this information is the breadth of the tasks sampled by the instrument. Instruments with a very narrow range of item content are less likely to be suited for detecting a variety of special needs than instruments sampling a number of different performance areas. The importance of wide CA ranges was also discussed in Chapter 5 and serves as a second evaluative criteria. Tests with wider CA applications allow for greater continuity in the developmental screening program across grade levels.

DESIRABLE FEATURES
OF A SCREENING INSTRUMENT

Group Test

Group screening tests are desirable from the standpoint that group administration reduces screening costs. Unfortunately, most group tests entail paper-pencil items which tap only a small sample of the behaviors that may reveal special needs. In the opinion of the present author, it is desirable to achieve a mix of group and individual tests in order to both increase the representativeness of the skills assessed and at the same time to keep costs to a minimum.

Teacher Administered

Except for speech screening, it is usually too costly to employ school psychologists, diagnosticians or other specialists to perform screening functions. There is an overwhelming demand for the counseling and diagnostic services of school psychologists and diagnosticians while at the same time there is an undersupply of those professionals on school staffs. Therefore, it is desirable for teachers to be able to perform the actual screening. Any test identified as suitable for administration by a parent or paraprofessional also received a check in the *Teacher Administration* column. It is assumed that a teacher might be responsible for supervising or somehow monitoring the administration of the instrument by the paraprofessional, parent, or volunteer.

Fast

Generally, group tests were rated "fast" unless the testing sessions exceeded, in total, 1½ hours. Individual tests were rated as "fast" if the testing time was approximately 20 minutes or less. These standards were not strictly adhered to, however, and a certain degree of judgment is reflected in the author's ratings on that criteria. The "fastness" of a test is a relative concept since no valid instrument gives an instant reading of the many special needs that students may display.

OK Preschool

If a test was intended for use with children under 4½ years of age, the test was judged adequate for use with preschool populations. In the opinion of the present author, appropriateness for preschool populations is a desirable feature because of the need to identify children early enough to provide sustained intervention over a longer period of time and before problems become compounded by the demands of formal schooling. The rating *OK Preschool* does not imply that the test ought to be used for this group, i.e. the items are valid and the test is adequately designed for use with young children. It only means that the test developers *claim* that the test can be used with children of ages as low as 4 – 6.

Non-Verbal Components

An instrument was rated as possessing the desirable feature *Non-Verbal Components* if the examinee's response to the test was non-verbal, such as pointing or gesturing or imitating a motor act, at least for some items. A similar rating was given if any of the items involved non-verbal stimuli such as pictures, objects, or designs. The presence of non-verbal components is important in a developmental screening test because many of the children who will be seen will display differences on verbal and non-verbal items. Variations between non-verbal and verbal areas may be of significance to those pursuing follow-up diagnosis. Also, the presence of non-verbal items serves to improve the morale and motivation of students who have problems dealing with verbal material and provides them with an opportunity for experiencing some success in the testing situation. In the event that a child cannot be tested in his native language, non-verbal items may provide some clues as to the need for more detailed follow-up.

Inexpensive

Inexpensive refers only to the cost of acquiring the tests and materials. One should note that a test which is very inexpensive to acquire may be very expensive to use in the long run. It would be advisable not to exclude any test from consideration solely on the basis of the fact that the materials themselves are expensive.This information has to be considered in the context of the entire instrument selection problem. The dollar costs (per 1977) of the test materials are contained in the Instrument Index (Appendix).

Standard Scores

Standard scores aid in the interpretation of test performance. Included among standard scores are grade equivalent, age equivalents, and percentiles. There are many standard scores. Standard scores inform the professional of the child's relative performance. In other words, they provide a type of yard stick for interpreting a child's performance. Standard scores are no better than the standardization population on which they are based. It is possible for a test to have standard score transformations that are based on very inadequate and/ or unrepresentative samples. This condition is not evaluated by the profiles. A total absence of standard scores, however, makes it exceedingly difficult to interpret individual performance.

Spanish Versions

Few developmental screening instruments are available in Spanish versions even though the Spanish speaking represent the second largest linguistic group in the United States, next to the English speaking. In some cases Spanish translations have been made of tests that were designed for English speaking children. Although this procedure represents an attempt to meet an important need, direct translations are not always adequate because of variations in concepts from one language to the other. Research shows that simple translations of tests from English into Spanish result in reductions in their reliability and validity (Simon and Joiner, 1976). Despite this problem, it is very desirable to make some provision for the Spanish speaking or other significant local linguistic group in a community screening program. It may be necessary to initiate this effort at the local level since even for Spanish, a major language spoken in the country, few instruments exist.

A check in the *Spanish Version* column of the instrument profiles only indicates that some provision has been made for administering the instrument to Spanish speaking children. This does not represent an endorsement of the instrument for use with that language group and provides no evaluative information regarding the adequacy of the instrument for that language group.

Disadvantaged

Despite extensive discussion in educational literature of the special problems of the disadvantaged in the area of assessment, few developmental screening instruments have been designed with special attention to the disadvantaged child's problems. Most developmental screening instruments fail to include a representative number of disadvantaged children in normative samples and rarely supply norms which are adjusted for the child's socio-economic background. To a large degree, special provisions for the disadvantaged in developmental screening instrument design are non-existent.

The reader will note, therefore, that few instruments receive a check in the *Disadvantaged* column, indicating that no special provisions were reportedly made in test development, norming, or scoring which would make the instrument more suitable for use with the disadvantaged child. The presence of a check in that column, as was the case for the *Spanish Version*, does not indicate that the attempt that may have been made to tailor the tests to the problems and characteristics of the disadvantaged were successful. It only means that some direct consideration, thought, and effort was given this issue as evidenced by the test manuals, or standardization samples.

SPECIAL NEEDS ASSESSED

Because of the problems described in the chapter on classification, instrument profiles include only indications of the broad areas of special need surveyed by the screening instrument. Generally, the profiles of special needs are based on a content analysis of the items contained in the instrument and the ascribed purposes of the test according to the developer.

There are very few consistencies among instruments in the vocabularies that are used to describe their purposes. The working definitions used by the present author in determining whether or not a test was *potentially* relevant to detecting a special need are as follows:

Social: assessments of a child's direct interactions with others, either child or adult; their extent, quality, and results. Typically, evidence is acquired through direct observation, rating scales used by adults such as parents, and for older children, self-reports.

Emotional: not easily separated from "social" since manifestations of emotional needs often appear in social interaction. Instrument content relating to emotional needs detect feelings about self and others reflected in statements made by the child or his/her approach to learning: e.g., negativism, easily discouraged, fear of success of failure, pre-occupation and lack of concentration.

Language: verbal communication and expressing ideas in words. This is distinct from articulation or problems relating to the physical production of speech sounds. Vocabulary, semantic knowledge, oral expression, are examples of specific subtest items assessing special needs in the area of language.

Concepts: emphasis is on general, broad understandings such as classification, relationships, numbers, time, causality, deductions, and inferences.

Speech: articulation proficiency, pronunciation of phonemes, the physical production of speech sounds, and intelligibility of speech are among the terms appearing in descriptions of screening instruments for assessing special needs in this area.

Visual: tasks involving eye-hand coordination, identification or interpretation of visual information, patterns, figures, etc. Visual acuity problems are not directly assessed by developmental screening instruments reviewed.

Auditory: interpreting and organizing sounds or words that are heard; being able to synthesize sounds as in sound blending, a skill necessary for profiting from a phonics program in reading. Tests that screen for physical or psychogenic hearing losses are not included.

Perceptual-Motor: motor behavior involving coordinating movements with auditory, factual or kinesthetic stimuli.

Self-Help: The general adaptive behavior of the individual; capacity for self-care; independence, knowledge and use of surrounding resources.

INSTRUMENT PROFILE CHART

The following 32 pages make up the *Instrument Profile Chart*, representing 137 screening instruments.

Instrument, Item Content and CA Range	Social	Emotional	Language	Concepts	Speech	Visual	Auditory	Perceptual-Motor	Self-Help	Disadvantaged	Spanish Version	Standard Scores	Inexpensive	Easy Scoring	Non-Verbal Cmpnts.	OK Pre-School	Fast	Teacher Admin.	Group Test
The ABC Inventory (3-6 to 6-6) — drawing, copying, folding, counting, memory, general information, colors, size and time concepts			+	+				+				+	+	+	+	+	+	+	
Adaptive Behavior Scales (3-0 to adult) — measures environmental coping ability of children and adults	+	+							+		rs		+		rs				
American School Reading Readiness Test (5-0 to 6-0) — picture vocabulary, discrimination of forms, letter form recognition, letter combination recognition, word recognition, word matching, following directions and memory for designs			+					+				+	+	+	+	+		+	+
Anton Brenner Developmental Gestalt Test of School Readiness (5-0 to 6-0) — number producing, number recognition, ten dot gestalt, sentence gestalt and draw-a-man			+					+				+	+		+		+	+	

c = communication   cr = criterion referenced   ct = composite for several tests   d/b = deaf/blind   exp = experimental edition

fs = appropriate for foreign speaking   ld = language disabled   nv = non-verbal   prs = parent rating scale   rs = rating scale   sh = severely handicapped

Instrument, Item Content and CA Range	Group Test	Teacher Admin.	Fast	OK Pre-School	Non-Verbal Cmpnts.	Easy Scoring	Inexpensive	Standard Scores	Spanish Version	Disadvantaged	Social	Emotional	Language	Concepts	Speech	Visual	Auditory	Perceptual-Motor	Self-Help
Arizona Articulation Proficiency Scale: Revised (3-0 to adult) — articulation proficiency, pronunciation of initial and final consonants, vowel sounds		+		+		+	+									+			
Assets: A Survey of Student's Educational Talents and Skills (4-0 to 12-0) — profile of academic aptitudes, motivational characteristics, creative thinking abilities, visual and performing arts talent and special interests	+	+	+	+	+	+			+	+	+	+	+			+			+
Bender Motor Gestalt Test (4-0 to 12-0) — non-verbal, visual perception items	+			+	+			+	nv									+	
Birth-Three Scale (0-1 to 3-0) — oral language (comprehension and expression), problem solving, social/personal and motor development		+	+	+	+	+		+			+	+	+	+				+	

c = communication   cr = criterion referenced   ct = composite for several tests   exp = experimental edition

fs = appropriate for foreign speaking   ld = language disabled   nv = non-verbal   prs = parent rating scale   d/b = deaf/blind   rs = rating scale   sh = severely handicapped

Instrument, Item Content and CA Range	Self-Help	Perceptual-Motor	Auditory	Visual	Speech	Concepts	Language	Emotional	Social	Disadvantaged	Spanish Version	Standard Scores	Inexpensive	Easy Scoring	Non-Verbal Cmpnts.	OK Pre-School	Fast	Teacher Admin.	Group Test
	Special Needs Assessed									**Desired Features**									
Boehm Test of Basic Concepts (4-0 to 8-0) space (location, direction, orientation and dimension), time and quantity (number)						+	+			+		+	+	+	+	+	+	+	+
Boyd Developmental Progress Scale (0-1 to 8-0) motor skills, communications skills, and self-sufficiency skills	+	+		+			+						+	+	+	+		+	
Burks Behavior Rating Scale (6-0 to 12-0) vegetative-autonomic, perceptual-discrimination, social-emotional		+						+	+		rs		+	+	rs	+	+		
Cain-Levine Social Competency Scales (5-0 to 13-0) self-help, initiative, social skills and communication	+						+	+	+		rs	+	+	+	rs	+		+	
Camelot Behavioral Checklist (3-0 to 13-0) checklist of child's behavioral skills	+							+	+		rs			+	rs	+		+	

c = communication   cr = criterion referenced   ct = composite for several tests   d/b = deaf/blind   exp = experimental edition

fs = appropriate for foreign speaking   ld = language disabled   nv = non-verbal   prs = parent rating scale   rs = rating scale   sh = severely handicapped

Instrument, Item Content and CA Range	Special Needs Assessed									Desired Features									
	Self-Help	Perceptual-Motor	Auditory	Visual	Speech	Concepts	Language	Emotional	Social	Disadvantaged	Spanish Version	Standard Scores	Inexpensive	Easy Scoring	Non-Verbal Cmpnts.	OK Pre-School	Fast	Teacher Admin.	Group Test
Carolina Developmental Profile (2-0 to 5-0) — fine motor, gross motor, perceptual reasoning, receptive and expressive language		+		+		+	+	+	+			cr		+	+	+		+	
Carrow Elicited Language Inventory (3-0 to 7-11) — specific linguistic structures							+				rs	+	+	+					
CCD Developmental Progress Scale (Experimental Form) (0-1 to 8-0) — direct observation or parent respondent scale assessing motor, interpersonal communication and self-sufficiency skills	+	+					+	+	+		rs		+	+	rs	+		+	
Child Behavior Rating Scale (5-0 to 8-0) — scale for assessing home, self, social, school and physical adjustment								+	+		rs		+		rs	rs	+	+	

c = communication   cr = criterion referenced   ct = composite for several tests   d/b = deaf/blind   exp = experimental edition

fs = appropriate for foreign speaking   ld = language disabled   nv = non-verbal   prs = parent rating scale   rs = rating scale   sh = severely handicapped

Instrument, Item Content and CA Range	Group Test	Teacher Admin.	Fast	OK Pre-School	Non-Verbal Cmpnts.	Easy Scoring	Inexpensive	Standard Scores	Spanish Version	Disadvantaged	Social	Emotional	Language	Concepts	Speech	Visual	Auditory	Perceptual-Motor	Self-Help
Children's Self-Social Construct Tests (Experimental Version) (3-0 to 8-0) — self-concept in the areas of dependency, esteem, realism as to color and size, social interest, minority identification and identification with close relations.			+	+	+	+	+			+	+	+							
Cincinnati Autonomy Test Battery (3-0 to 6-0) — social competency, curiosity, innovative behavior, impulse control, reflectivity, incidental and intentional learning, persistance, resistance, task competence and verbalization		+		+	+					+	+	+	+	+					+
Circus (4-0 to 6-0) — measures language competencies (understanding of and production of language), perception, information processing and experience, divergent production, interest and styles, test taking behavior and a description of the child's educational environment	+	+		+	+	+							+			+	+	+	

c = communication   cr = criterion referenced   ct = composite for several tests   d/b = deaf/blind   exp = experimental edition

fs = appropriate for foreign speaking   ld = language disabled   nv = non-verbal   prs = parent rating scale   rs = rating scale   sh = severely handicapped

Instrument, Item Content and CA Range	Self-Help	Perceptual-Motor	Auditory	Visual	Speech	Concepts	Language	Emotional	Social	Disadvantaged	Spanish Version	Standard Scores	Inexpensive	Easy Scoring	Non-Verbal Cmpnts.	OK Pre-School	Fast	Teacher Admin.	Group Test
Cognitive Skills Assessment Battery (3-0 to 6-0) orientation and familiarity with the environment, coordination, discrimination, memory, comprehension and concept formation		+	+	+		+	+					cr	+	+	+	+		+	
Columbia Mental Maturity Scale (3-6 to 10-0) classification skills, pictorial stimuli						+					nv				+	+			
Communicative Evaluation Chart from Infancy to Five Years (0-3 to 5-0) parent interview, child responses, language, physical growth and development		+	+	+		+	+				rs	+	+	+	rs	+		+	
Comprehensive Identification Process (CIP) (2-6 to 5-6) screening test including: fine motor, gross motor, cognitive-verbal, speech/expressive language, hearing, vision, social/affective and medical		+			+	+	+	+	+						+	+		+	

c = communication   cr = criterion referenced   ct = composite for several tests   d/b = deaf/blind   exp = experimental edition
fs = appropriate for foreign speaking   ld = language disabled   nv = non-verbal   prs = parent rating scale   rs = rating scale   sh = severely handicapped

Instrument, Item Content and CA Range	Group Test	Teacher Admin.	Fast	OK Pre-School	Non-Verbal Cmpnts.	Easy Scoring	Inexpensive	Standard Scores	Spanish Version	Disadvantaged	Social	Emotional	Language	Concepts	Speech	Visual	Auditory	Perceptual-Motor	Self-Help
Contemporary School Readiness Test (5-0 to 6-6) — visual discrimination, auditory discrimination, listening comprehension, writing ability to learn to read words, understanding of numbers and background for understanding science, health and social studies	+	+			+		+	+					+	+		+	+		
Cooperative Preschool Inventory (3-0 to 6-0) — basic information and vocabulary, number concepts, concepts of size, motion, color and time, social function, object classification, visual-motor performance, following instructions and independence and self-help		+		+	+	+	+	+		+			+	+		+		+	+
Dailey Language Facility Test (3-0 to 17-0) — describing pictures: errors in standard English pronunciation or English usage		+		+			+		+	+			+		+				

c = communication   cr = criterion referenced   ct = composite for several tests   d/b = deaf/blind   exp = experimental edition

fs = appropriate for foreign speaking   ld = language disabled   nv = non-verbal   prs = parent rating scale   rs = rating scale   sh = severely handicapped

Instrument, Item Content and CA Range	Group Test	Teacher Admin.	Fast	OK Pre-School	Non-Verbal Cmpnts.	Easy Scoring	Inexpensive	Standard Scores	Spanish Version	Disadvantaged	Social	Emotional	Language	Concepts	Speech	Visual	Auditory	Perceptual-Motor	Self-Help
					Desired Features								Special Needs Assessed						
Del Rio Language Screening Test (3-0 to 6-11) English and Spanish language screening: receptive vocabulary, sentence repetition-length, sentence repetition-complexity, oral commands and story comprehension		+		+	+		+	+	+				+						
Denver Articulation Screening Exam (DASE) (2-6 to 7-0) articulation development: ability to pronounce 30 sound elements, intelligently in conversation		+	+	+			+	+							+				
Denver Developmental Screening Test (0-1 to 6-0) assesses delays in motor, physical, social and language development		+	+	+	+	+	+				+	+	+	+				+	
Denver Prescreening Developmental Questionnaire (0-3 to 6-0) prescreening instrument identifying individuals for follow-up screening with Denver Developmental Screening Test		+		+	rs	+	+				+	+	+					+	

c = communication   cr = criterion referenced   ct = composite for several tests   d/b = deaf/blind   exp = experimental edition
fs = appropriate for foreign speaking   ld = language disabled   nv = non-verbal   prs = parent rating scale   rs = rating scale   sh = severely handicapped

Special Needs Assessed									Desired Features											Instrument, Item Content and CA Range
Self-Help	Perceptual-Motor	Auditory	Visual	Speech	Concepts	Language	Emotional	Social	Disadvantaged	Spanish Version	Standard Scores	Inexpensive	Easy Scoring	Non-Verbal Cmpnts.	OK Pre-School	Fast	Teacher Admin.	Group Test		
	+	+	+		+	+				fs	+	+		+	+		+			**Detroit Tests of Learning Aptitude (3-0 to adult)** — 19 subtests including reasoning and comprehension, practical judgment, verbal ability, time and space relationships, number ability, auditory attentive ability, visual attentive ability and motor ability
+	+				+	+	+	+		rs	rs	+		rs	+		+			**Developmental Guidelines (3-0 to 6-0)** — task lists by age for: fine and gross motor, cognition, self-help and social development
	+			+	+	+	+	+						+	+		+			**Developmental Indicator for the Assessment of Learning (DIAL) (2-6 to 5-6)** — gross motor, fine motor, concepts, communication and social/emotional development
	+					+	+	+				+	+	+	+	+	+			**Developmental Key for Assessing Children's Growth (3-0 to 6-0)** — teacher ratings of: social, emotional, physical, language and cognitive development

c = communication   cr = criterion referenced   ct = composite for several tests   d/b = deaf/blind   exp = experimental edition
fs = appropriate for foreign speaking   ld = language disabled   nv = non-verbal   prs = parent rating scale   rs = rating scale   sh = severely handicapped

Instrument, Item Content and CA Range	Group Test	Teacher Admin.	Fast	OK Pre-School	Non-Verbal Cmpnts.	Easy Scoring	Inexpensive	Standard Scores	Spanish Version	Disadvantaged	Social	Emotional	Language	Concepts	Speech	Visual	Auditory	Perceptual-Motor	Self-Help
							Desired Features						**Special Needs Assessed**						
Developmental Profile (0-6 to 12-0) developmental interview to assess: physical, self-help, social, academic and communication development		+		+	rs	+	+	rs	rs		+	+	+					+	+
Developmental Screening Inventory (DSI) (0-1 to 1-6) serial observations by parents of: gross motor, fine motor, language, personal, social and adaptive development	+	+	+	+	+	+	+				+	+	+					+	
Developmental Test of Visual Motor Integration (2-0 to 15-0) screening for visual perceptual or motor behavior problems; geometric figures arranged in order of increasing difficulty	+	+		+	+		+	+	nv							+		+	
Developmental Test of Visual Perception (3-0 to 8-0) perceptual skills test: eye motor coordination, figure ground, constancy of shape, position in space and spatial relationships		+		+	+		+	+	nv							+		+	

c = communication   cr = criterion referenced   ct = composite for several tests   exp = experimental edition
fs = appropriate for foreign speaking   ld = language disabled   nv = non-verbal   prs = parent rating scale   sh = severely handicapped
d/b = deaf/blind   rs = rating scale

Instrument, Item Content and CA Range	Self-Help	Perceptual-Motor	Auditory	Visual	Speech	Concepts	Language	Emotional	Social	Disadvantaged	Spanish Version	Standard Scores	Inexpensive	Easy Scoring	Non-Verbal Cmpnts.	OK Pre-School	Fast	Teacher Admin.	Group Test
Early Childhood Assessment: A Criterion-Referenced Screening Device (3-6 to 7-0) — a criterion-referenced, developmental test: auditory, visual, motor and verbal development		+	+	+			+					cr	+	+	+	+		+	
Early Detection Inventory (3-0 to 6-0) — readiness in: social and emotional development, physical development, motor development and intellectual development		+					+	+	+				+		+	+			
Early Education Screening Test – Battery of Basic Skills Development (4-0 to 6-0) — motor, auditory, visual, motor coordination, retention, language and cognition		+	+	+			+	+				ct			+	+		+	
Early Identification Screening Inventory (5-0 to adult) — teacher rating of: visual motor, speech and hearing, physical, visual, and psycho-motor and behavior		+		+	+		+	+	+				+		rs				

c = communication   cr = criterion referenced   ct = composite for several tests   d/b = deaf/blind   exp = experimental edition
fs = appropriate for foreign speaking   ld = language disabled   nv = non-verbal   prs = parent rating scale   rs = rating scale   sh = severely handicapped

Instrument, Item Content and CA Range	Self-Help	Perceptual-Motor	Auditory	Visual	Speech	Concepts	Language	Emotional	Social	Disadvantaged	Spanish Version	Standard Scores	Inexpensive	Easy Scoring	Non-Verbal Cmpnts.	OK Pre-School	Fast	Teacher Admin.	Group Test
The Educational Developmental Program, Kit I (4-0 to 7-0) — detects strengths and weaknesses in: information, language development, auditory discrimination, perception, fine and gross motor functioning and number concepts		+	+	+		+	+							+	+	+		+	
Eliot-Pearson Screening Inventory (4-0 to 6-0) — evaluates perceptual, cognitive, language and motor development		+		+			+						+	+	+	+	+	+	
Evanston Early Identification Scale (Field Research Edition) (5-0 to 6-3) — targeted to: emotional or perceptual difficulties, a human figure drawing test		+		+				+	+		nv		+	+	+			+	
Fairview Behavior Evaluation Battery for the Mentally Retarded (0-1 to 10-0) — checklists for: self-help, social skills, language evolution and problem behavior	+						+	+	+		rs	+		+	rs			+	

c = communication   cr = criterion referenced   ct = composite for several tests   exp = experimental edition
fs = appropriate for foreign speaking   ld = language disabled   nv = non-verbal   prs = parent rating scale   d/b = deaf/blind   rs = rating scale   sh = severely handicapped

Instrument, Item Content and CA Range

First Grade Screening Test (FGST) (4-6 to 6-0)
screens for: intellectual deficiency, central nervous system dysfunction and emotional disturbance

A General Screening Instrument
teacher ratings of academic and behavioral items

Gessell Developmental Examination (5-0 to 10-0)
assesses developmental level: writing name, address, numbers, copying figures and forms, incomplete man, right and left subtests, matching forms, memory for designs, visual projective test and naming animals

Gessell Developmental Schedules (0-1 to 6-0)
estimates of developmental level in: motor development, language, adaptive behavior and personal-social adjustment

Instrument	Special Needs Assessed									Desired Features									
	Self-Help	Perceptual-Motor	Auditory	Visual	Speech	Concepts	Language	Emotional	Social	Disadvantaged	Spanish Version	Standard Scores	Inexpensive	Easy Scoring	Non-Verbal Cmpts.	OK Pre-School	Fast	Teacher Admin.	Group Test
First Grade Screening Test (FGST)		+					+	+	+			+	+	+	+		+	+	+
A General Screening Instrument						+	+	+	+			rs	+		rs			+	
Gessell Developmental Examination		+		+			+	+	+			+	+	+	+				
Gessell Developmental Schedules	+	+					+	+	+		rs		+	+	rs	+			

c = communication   cr = criterion referenced   ct = composite for several tests   exp = experimental edition
fs = appropriate for foreign speaking   ld = language disabled   nv = non-verbal   prs = parent rating scale
d/b = deaf/blind   rs = rating scale   sh = severely handicapped

Instrument, Item Content and CA Range	Group Test	Teacher Admin.	Fast	OK Pre-School	Non-Verbal Cmpnts.	Easy Scoring	Inexpensive	Standard Scores	Spanish Version	Disadvantaged	Social	Emotional	Language	Concepts	Speech	Visual	Auditory	Perceptual-Motor	Self-Help
Goldman-Fristoe-Woodcock Auditory Skills Test Battery (3-8 to adult) auditory selective attention test, diagnostic auditory discrimination test, auditory memory test and sound-symbol-test		+	+	+		+	+										+		
Goodenough Harris Drawing Test (3-0 to 15-0) draw-a-man, draw-a-woman, draw-yourself	+	+	+	+	+		+	+	nv		+	+	+	+				+	
Harris Tests of Lateral Dominance (7-0 to adult) knowledge of right and left, hand preferences, simultaneous writing, handwriting, tapping, dealing cards, strength of grip, monocular tests and binocular tests		+			+		+	+	nv									+	
Houston Test for Language Development (0-6 to 6-0) two levels; an observation schedule and: vocabulary, identification of body parts and gestures, geometric drawings, design, counting and a language sample				+	+								+	+				+	

c = communication   cr = criterion referenced   ct = composite for several tests   d/b = deaf/blind   exp = experimental edition
fs = appropriate for foreign speaking   ld = language disabled   nv = non-verbal   prs = parent rating scale   rs = rating scale   sh = severely handicapped

Instrument, Item Content and CA Range	Self-Help	Perceptual-Motor	Auditory	Visual	Speech	Concepts	Language	Emotional	Social	Disadvantaged	Spanish Version	Standard Scores	Inexpensive	Easy Scoring	Non-Verbal Cmpnts.	OK Pre-School	Fast	Teacher Admin.	Group Test
Infant Behavior Inventory (1-0 to 3-0) includes: attentiveness, concentration, distractibility fatigue, perseverance, verbal expressiveness and others					+			+	+		rs		+		rs	+		+	
Infant Intelligence Scale (0-3 to 2-6) a downward extension of the revised Stanfor-Binet scale						+	+					+	+	+	+	+	+		
Initial Screening Checklist (6-0 to 14-0) self-control, introversion, interpersonal behavior, anxiety, coordination, attention, language and time and space orientation		+				+	+	+	+		rs		+	+	rs			+	
Inter-American Services: Test of General Ability, Preschool Level (4-0 to 5-0) English or Spanish measure of readiness: oral vocabulary, number, association and classification						+	+				+	+	+	+	+	+		+	

c = communication   cr = criterion referenced   ct = composite for several tests   exp = experimental edition

fs = appropriate for foreign speaking   ld = language disabled   nv = non-verbal   prs = parent rating scale   d/b = deaf/blind   rs = rating scale   sh = severely handicapped

Instrument, Item Content and CA Range	Self-Help	Perceptual-Motor	Auditory	Visual	Speech	Concepts	Language	Emotional	Social	Disadvantaged	Spanish Version	Standard Scores	Inexpensive	Easy Scoring	Non-Verbal Cmprts.	OK Pre-School	Fast	Teacher Admin.	Group Test
Inventory for Language Abilities (4-0 to 18-0) auditory reception, visual reception, auditory association, visual association, verbal expression, manual expression, auditory memory, visual closure, auditory closure and sound blending		+	+	+			+				rs		+	+	rs	+		+	
Inventory of Readiness Skills (3-0 to 7-0) auditory memory, word discrimination, body awareness, locational and directional concepts, color discrimination, visual perception, letters and letter names		+	+	+		+	+						+	+	+	+	+	+	
Jansky Screening Index (5-0 to 6-0) Gestalt, word matching, letter naming, picture naming and sentence memory		+	+	+			+					+	+		+		+	+	
Kindergarten Auditory Screening Test (4-6 to 6-0) listening for speech against a background of noise, synthesizing phonemes into words and telling whether words in pairs are the same or different			+										+	+			+	+	+

c = communication   cr = criterion referenced   ct = composite for several tests   exp = experimental edition
fs = appropriate for foreign speaking   ld = language disabled   nv = non-verbal   prs = parent rating scale   d/b = deaf/blind   rs = rating scale   sh = severely handicapped

Instrument, Item Content and CA Range	Self-Help	Perceptual-Motor	Auditory	Visual	Speech	Concepts	Language	Emotional	Social	Disadvantaged	Spanish Version	Standard Scores	Inexpensive	Easy Scoring	Non-Verbal Cmpnts.	OK Pre-School	Fast	Teacher Admin.	Group Test
Kindergarten Evaluation of Learning Potential (KELP) (4-6 to 6-0) skipping, color identification, bead design, bolt board, block design, calendar, number boards, safety signs, writing a name, auditory perception, social interaction		+	+	+			+		+			+		+	+			+	+
Language Facility Test (3-0 to 15-0) picture-elicited language scored for complexity and organization							+			+		+	+	+		+	+	+	
Language and Learning Disorders of the Pre-Academic Child measures language and cognitive development		+	+				+	+	+				+			+			
Laradon Articulation Scale (1-0 to 8-6) picture articulation test based on phonemic taxonomy			+		+							+				+		+	
Lexington Developmental Scale (Short Form) (0-11 to 6-0) motor, language, cognitive, emotional and personal-social development		+				+	+	+	+				+	+	+	+			

c = communication   cr = criterion referenced   ct = composite for several tests   d/b = deaf/blind   exp = experimental edition
fs = appropriate for foreign speaking   ld = language disabled   nv = non-verbal   prs = parent rating scale   rs = rating scale   sh = severely handicapped

Instrument, Item Content and CA Range	Group Test	Teacher Admin.	Fast	OK Pre-School	Non-Verbal Cmpnts.	Easy Scoring	Inexpensive	Standard Scores	Spanish Version	Disadvantaged	Social	Emotional	Language	Concepts	Speech	Visual	Auditory	Perceptual-Motor	Self-Help
The Magic Kingdom: A Preschool Screening Program (3-0 to 6-0) — motor, visual, auditory, language, conceptual, social-emotional and self-help functioning		+		+	+	+					+	+	+	+		+	+	+	+
A Manual for the Assessment of a "Deaf-Blind" Multiple Handicapped Child — Revised Edition — checklist of: self-help skills, social, gross motor, fine motor, communication and cognition		+	+	+	+		+		db	db	+	+	c	+				+	+
Maturity Level for School Entrance and Reading Readiness (5-0 to 6-6) — inventory of: body coordination, eye-hand coordination, speech and language comprehension, personal independence and social cooperation		+		+	rs	+	+		rs	rs	+	+	+	+	+			+	+
Maxfield-Bucholz Scale of Social Maturity with Pre-School — direct observations of: self-help, communication, socialization, locomotion and occupation		+		+	rs		+		rs		+	+	+			+			+

c = communication   ct = composite for several tests   cr = criterion referenced   exp = experimental edition

fs = appropriate for foreign speaking   ld = language disabled   nv = non-verbal   prs = parent rating scale   d/b = deaf/blind   rs = rating scale   sh = severely handicapped

	Special Needs Assessed									Desired Features										Instrument, Item Content and CA Range
	Self-Help	Perceptual-Motor	Auditory	Visual	Speech	Concepts	Language	Emotional	Social	Disadvantaged	Spanish Version	Standard Scores	Inexpensive	Easy Scoring	Non-Verbal Cmpnts.	OK Pre-School	Fast	Teacher Admin.	Group Test	
		+		+			+	+	+				+		+		+	+		**Meeting Street School Screening Test** — behavior rating scale for: motor patterning, visual-perceptual-motion and language; ten behavioral observation ratings
		+		+							nv		+		+		+			**Memory-for-Designs Test** — perceptual-motor coordination
		+				+	+	+	+		rs		+	+	rs	+		+		**Memphis Comprehensive Developmental Scale** — rating scale: personal-social, gross motor, fine motor, language and perceptual-cognitive development
	+	+					+	+	+		prs		+	+	prs	+		prs		**Minnesota Child Development Inventory** — mother observes and rates: general development, gross motor, fine motor, expressive language, comprehension-conceptual, situation comprehension, self-help and personal-social development

c = communication   cr = criterion referenced   ct = composite for several tests   exp = experimental edition
fs = appropriate for foreign speaking   ld = language disabled   nv = non-verbal   prs = parent rating scale   sh = severely handicapped
d/b = deaf/blind   rs = rating scale

Instrument, Item Content and CA Range	Group Test	Teacher Admin.	Fast	OK Pre-School	Non-Verbal Cmpnts.	Easy Scoring	Inexpensive	Standard Scores	Spanish Version	Disadvantaged	Social	Emotional	Language	Concepts	Speech	Visual	Auditory	Perceptual-Motor	Self-Help
Missouri Children's Picture Series (5-0 to 6-0) — non-verbal personality test: conformity, masculinity-feminity, maturity, aggression, inhibition, activity level, sleep disturbance and somatization	+	+	+		+		+	+	nv		+	+							
Motor Free Visual Perception Test (4-0 to 8-0) — visual-perceptual abilities without a motor component: visual discrimination, figure-ground, spatial relations, visual closure and visual memory		+		+	+	+	+	+	nv	nv				+		+			
Motor Problems Inventory (3-0 to 11-0) — small muscle coordination, laterality and gross motor coordination			+	+	+		+		rs									+	
Move-Grow-Learn (Movement Skills Survey) (3-0 to 9-0) — examiner's observations of child in classroom, playground and gymnasium activities		+	+	+	+		+		nv									+	
Northwestern Syntax Screening Test (3-0 to 8-0) — measures delayed syntactic development			+	+			+						+						

c = communication   cr = criterion referenced   ct = composite for several tests   d/b = deaf/blind   exp = experimental edition
fs = appropriate for foreign speaking   ld = language disabled   nv = non-verbal   prs = parent rating scale   rs = rating scale   sh = severely handicapped

Instrument, Item Content and CA Range	Self-Help	Perceptual-Motor	Auditory	Visual	Speech	Concepts	Language	Emotional	Social	Disadvantaged	Spanish Version	Standard Scores	Inexpensive	Easy Scoring	Non-Verbal Cmpnts.	OK Pre-School	Fast	Teacher Admin.	Group Test
Oseretsky Test of Motor Proficiency (4-0 to 16-0) general static coordination, motor-speed, simultaneous voluntary movements and performance without extraneous movements		+									nv		+		+	+		+	
Parent Readiness Evaluation of Pre-Schoolers (PREP) (4-0 to 6-0) parents rate child's development in verbal and performance areas		+	+	+			+				prs	prs	+	+	prs	+	+	prs	
Photo Articulation Test (3-0 to 12-0) articulation of all consonants, vowels and common blends within the initial, medial and final positions as well as in isolation					+								+	+		+	+	+	
Piers-Harris Children's Self-Concept Scale (7-0 to 17-0) self-ratings using 60 declarative statements								+	+			+	+						+
Pre-Academic Learning Inventory (4-6 to 6-0) criterion-referenced test of nine areas of development		+	+	+	+	+	+					+	+	+	+		+	+	
Predictive Screening Test of Articulation (5-0 to 6-0) assesses need for misarticulation therapy					+								+						

c = communication   cr = criterion referenced   ct = composite for several tests   d/b = deaf/blind   exp = experimental edition

fs = appropriate for foreign speaking   ld = language disabled   nv = non-verbal   prs = parent rating scale   rs = rating scale   sh = severely handicapped

Instrument, Item Content and CA Range	Self-Help	Perceptual-Motor	Auditory	Visual	Speech	Concepts	Language	Emotional	Social	Disadvantaged	Spanish Version	Standard Scores	Inexpensive	Easy Scoring	Non-Verbal Cmpnts.	OK Pre-School	Fast	Teacher Admin.	Group Test
Preprimary Profile (Introduction to My Child) (3-0 to 6-0) — parent rates child in: self-care, social behavior, skill development, language development and previous experience	+							+	+		prs	+	+	+	prs	+	+	prs	
Pre-School Attainment Record Research Edition (0-6 to 7-0) — parent or teacher rating of physical, social and intellectual development		+				+		+	+		prs		+	+	rs	+	+	+	
Pre-reading Screening Procedures (5-0 to 6-0) — test evaluates child's auditory, visual and visual-motor capabilities: letter forms, recognition, recall, copying, auditory discrimination, letter knowledge		+	+	+		+	+						+	+	+	+	+	+	+
Preschool Behavior Questionnaire: Manual and Questionnaire Set (3-0 to 6-0) — interviewer seeks information from secondary source on: hostility, anxiety, and hyperactivity								+	+			+	+		rs	+		+	

Column group headings: **Special Needs Assessed** (Self-Help, Perceptual-Motor, Auditory, Visual, Speech, Concepts, Language, Emotional, Social); **Desired Features** (Disadvantaged, Spanish Version, Standard Scores, Inexpensive, Easy Scoring, Non-Verbal Cmpnts., OK Pre-School, Fast, Teacher Admin., Group Test).

c = communication   cr = criterion referenced   ct = composite for several tests   exp = experimental edition
fs = appropriate for foreign speaking   ld = language disabled   nv = non-verbal   prs = parent rating scale   d/b = deaf/blind   rs = rating scale   sh = severely handicapped

Instrument, Item Content and CA Range	Special Needs Assessed									Desired Features									
	Self-Help	Perceptual-Motor	Auditory	Visual	Speech	Concepts	Language	Emotional	Social	Disadvantaged	Spanish Version	Standard Scores	Inexpensive	Easy Scoring	Non-Verbal Cmpnts.	OK Pre-School	Fast	Teacher Admin.	Group Test
Preschool Language Scale (1-6 to 7-0) — scale measures auditory comprehension and verbal ability			+		+		+				ld	+	+	+	+	+			
Preschool Screening Survey (3-5 to 6-6) — language-cognition, visual motor conceptualization, visual discrimination, motor coordination, numbers and digit span		+		+		+	+						+	+	+	+	+	+	+
Preschool Screening System (3-0 to 5-4) — parent questionnaire on child's language, visual-motor, body awareness and control skills		+		+		+	+		+			+	+	+	+	+		+	
Primary Academic Sentiment Scale (4-4 to 7-3) — test of motivation for learning: maturity, parental dependency, preferred activities, attitudes and behaviors								+	+			+	+	+	+		+	+	+
Primary Self-Concept Inventory (4-0 to 10-0) — English or Spanish inventory: social-self, personal-self and intellectual-self								+	+		+		+	+	+	+		+	+

c = communication cr = criterion referenced ct = composite for several tests exp = experimental edition
fs = appropriate for foreign speaking ld = language disabled nv = non-verbal prs = parent rating scale d/b = deaf/blind rs = rating scale sh = severely handicapped

Instrument, Item Content and CA Range	Group Test	Teacher Admin.	Fast	OK Pre-School	Non-Verbal Cmptrs.	Easy Scoring	Inexpensive	Standard Scores	Spanish Version	Disadvantaged	Social	Emotional	Language	Concepts	Speech	Visual	Auditory	Perceptual-Motor	Self-Help
	Desired Features										**Special Needs Assessed**								
Progress Assessment Charts of Social Development – Form I (Third Edition) and Form II (Second Edition) — social skills of profoundly mentally retarded and trainable mentally retarded children and adults: self-help, communication, socialization and occupation		+	+		rs	+	+		rs		+	+	+	+					+
Purdue Perceptual Motor Survey (6-0 to 10-0) — perceptual-motor test of laterality, perceptual-motor matching, and directionality		+			+		+											+	
Quick Neurological Screening Test (4-0 to 18-0) — assesses emotional, intellectual, sensory motor development, muscle coordination, readiness for number concepts and auditory-visual perception	+		+	+	+		+		rs		+	+	+			+	+	+	
Quick Screening Scale of Mental Development (0-6 to 10-0) — ratings in: body coordination, manual performance, speech and language, listening, attention, number concepts, play interests and general mental level				+	+		+	+			+	+	+	+	+		+		

c = communication   cr = criterion referenced   ct = composite for several tests   d/b = deaf/blind   exp = experimental edition

fs = appropriate for foreign speaking   ld = language disabled   nv = non-verbal   prs = parent rating scale   rs = rating scale   sh = severely handicapped

Instrument, Item Content and CA Range	Group Test	Teacher Admin.	Fast	OK Pre-School	Non-Verbal Cmpnts.	Easy Scoring	Inexpensive	Standard Scores	Spanish Version	Disadvantaged	Social	Emotional	Language	Concepts	Speech	Visual	Auditory	Perceptual-Motor	Self-Help
Quick Test (2-0 to adult) perceptual-verbal intelligence test			+	+		+	+						+						
Quick Word Test (9-0 to adult) a quick and inexpensive measure of general ability		+	+	+	+	+	+	+					+						
Rapid Developmental Screening Checklist (0-1 to 5-0) observational checklist measuring: language development, motor development, self-concept and behavior		+	+	+	rs	+	+				+	+	+		+				
Receptive-Expressive Emergent Language Scale (REEL) (0-1 to 3-0) measures receptive, expressive, and inner language development				+	rs								+						
Reynell Developmental Language Scales (1-0 to 5-0) developmental language scale of verbal comprehension and expressive language		+		+	+	+	+	+					+						
Riley Articulation and Language Test (4-0 to 7-0) measures articulation loss, language loss and language function			+	+		+	+	+					+		+				

c = communication   cr = criterion referenced   ct = composite for several tests   exp = experimental edition
fs = appropriate for foreign speaking   ld = language disabled   nv = non-verbal   prs = parent rating scale   rs = rating scale   sh = severely handicapped   d/b = deaf/blind

Instrument, Item Content and CA Range	Self-Help	Perceptual-Motor	Auditory	Visual	Speech	Concepts	Language	Emotional	Social	Disadvantaged	Spanish Version	Standard Scores	Inexpensive	Easy Scoring	Non-Verbal Cmprts.	OK Pre-School	Fast	Teacher Admin.	Group Test
Riley Preschool Developmental Screening Inventory (3-0 to 6-0) copy designs and draw a person		+		+		+						+	+	+	+	+	+	+	
Rosner Perceptual Survey (6-0 to 10-0) test of perceptual-motor dysfunctions: general status, word repetition, near visual acuity, steropsis, auditory organization, developmental drawing cover test, near point of convergence, pursuits, retinoscopy, motor skills, body image, rhythmic hop and tap, split-form board, auditory-visual, tactual-visual and Rutgers Drawing Test		+	+	+			+						exp		+		+		
Rosner-Richman Perceptual Survey (6-0 to 10-0) test of perceptual-motor dysfunctions: general status, word repetition, auditory organization, developmental drawing, motor skills, body image, rhythmic hop and tap, auditory visual and Rutgers Drawing Test		+	+	+			+						exp		+	+	+		
School Entrance Checklist (4-0 to 5-0) parent checklist including: early developmental history, medical history and observations concerning child's readiness for school						+	+	+	+		prs		+		prs +	+	prs +	prs	

c = communication   cr = criterion referenced   ct = composite for several tests   d/b = deaf/blind   exp = experimental edition

fs = appropriate for foreign speaking   ld = language disabled   nv = non-verbal   prs = parent rating scale   rs = rating scale   sh = severely handicapped

Instrument, Item Content and CA Range	Group Test	Teacher Admin.	Fast	OK Pre-School	Non-Verbal Cmpnts.	Easy Scoring	Inexpensive	Standard Scores	Spanish Version	Disadvantaged	Social	Emotional	Language	Concepts	Speech	Visual	Auditory	Perceptual-Motor	Self-Help
School Readiness Checklist — Ready or Not (4-0 to 5-0) scale for use by parents includes: age and physical development, general motor adeptness, memory and attention span, comprehension and reasoning, visual-perceptual skills, general knowledge and general emotional-social maturity		prs	+	+	prs	+	+				+	+	+			+		+	
School Readiness Survey (4-0 to 6-0) parent-administered device: number concepts, form discrimination, color naming, symbol matching, speaking vocabulary, listening vocabulary, general information		prs		+	prs	+	+				+	+	+	+		+			
Screening Test of Academic Readiness (STAR) (4-0 to 6-5) group screening test includes: picture vocabulary, letter, picture completion, copying, picture description, human figure drawing, relationships, numbers	+	+	+	+	+		+	+		+	+	+	+	+		+		+	

c = communication   cr = criterion referenced   ct = composite for several tests   d/b = deaf/blind   exp = experimental edition
fs = appropriate for foreign speaking   ld = language disabled   nv = non-verbal   prs = parent rating scale   rs = rating scale   sh = severely handicapped

Instrument, Item Content and CA Range	Group Test	Teacher Admin.	Fast	OK Pre-School	Non-Verbal Cmprts.	Easy Scoring	Inexpensive	Standard Scores	Spanish Version	Disadvantaged	Social	Emotional	Language	Concepts	Speech	Visual	Auditory	Perceptual-Motor	Self-Help
Screening Test for the Assignment of Remedial Treatment (START) (4-6 to 6-5) — group test assessing: visual memory, auditory memory, visual-motor coordination and visual discrimination	+	+	+		+	+	+	+		+						+	+	+	
Screening Test for Auditory Comprehension of Language (3-0 to 6-0) — screening test for: knowledge of vocabulary, morphology and syntax	+		+	+	+	+	+	+	+				+						
Sequenced Inventory of Communication Development (0-4 to 4-0) — measures expressive language, length, grammatic and syntactic structures of verbal output, articulation and receptive language				+	+ rs	+							+		+				
Slingerland Screening Tests for Identifying Children with Specific Language Disability (5-0 to 12-0) — assesses perceptual-motor development, echolalia	+	+			+		+						+			+	+	+	

c = communication   cr = criterion referenced   ct = composite for several tests   exp = experimental edition
fs = appropriate for foreign speaking   ld = language disabled   nv = non-verbal   prs = parent rating scale   d/b = deaf/blind   rs = rating scale   sh = severely handicapped

Self-Help	Perceptual-Motor	Auditory	Visual	Speech	Concepts	Language	Emotional	Social	Disadvantaged	Spanish Version	Standard Scores	Inexpensive	Easy Scoring	Non-Verbal Cmpnts.	OK Pre-School	Fast	Teacher Admin.	Group Test	Instrument, Item Content and CA Range
																			Special Needs Assessed / **Desired Features**
	+										+	+		+	+	+			**Southern California Perceptual-Motor Tests (4-0 to 8-0)** assesses children's perceptual-motor functioning: imitation of postures, crossing midline of body, bilateral motor coordination, right-left discrimination, standing balance — eyes open and eyes closed
	+	+	+			+						+		+		+	+		**Specific Language Disability Test (11-0 to 14-0)** assesses perceptual motor functioning: visual discrimination, visual memory, visual motor coordination, comprehension, auditory discrimination, auditory-visual coordination and auditory motor coordination
			+		+	+					+	+	+	+		+			**Springle School Readiness Screening Test (4-0 to 6-9)** parent interveiw to obtain information on: verbal comprehension, awareness of size relationships, visual discrimination, reasoning ability, numbers concept, comprehension of analogies, information background and spatial relationships
+	+					+	+	+	sh			+	+	rs	+		+		**The TARC Assessment System (3-0 to 16-0)** observations of child's performance in: self-help, motor, communication and social development

c = communication   cr = criterion referenced   ct = composite for several tests   exp = experimental edition
fs = appropriate for foreign speaking   ld = language disabled   nv = non-verbal   prs = parent rating scale   sh = severely handicapped
d/b = deaf/blind   rs = rating scale

Instrument, Item Content and CA Range	Self-Help	Perceptual-Motor	Auditory	Visual	Speech	Concepts	Language	Emotional	Social	Disadvantaged	Spanish Version	Standard Scores	Inexpensive	Easy Scoring	Non-Verbal Cmpnts.	OK Pre-School	Fast	Teacher Admin.	Group Test
Templin-Darley Tests of Articulation (3-0 to 8-0) — screening portion assesses child's general articulation adequacy					+							cr	+			+	+		
Test of Basic Experiences (General Concepts Section) Is Used as a General Screening Device (3-0 to 7-0) — includes language, mathematics, science, social studies and general concepts; general concepts subtest used for screening						+	+			+	+	+	+	+	+	+	+	+	+
Test of Nonverbal Auditory Discrimination (TENVAD) (5-0 to 8-0) — test of auditory discrimination: discrimination of pitch, loudness, rhythm, duration and timbre			+							+	nv	cr	+	+	+		+	+	+
Utah Test of Language Development (0-9 to 16-0) — measures expressive and receptive language skills							+						+	+	+	+			
Vane Kindergarten Test (4-0 to 6-11) — visual-motor, vocabulary and draw-a-man		+		+			+	+	+			+	+		+	+	+	+	+

Instrument, Item Content and CA Range	Special Needs Assessed									Desired Features									
	Self-Help	Perceptual-Motor	Auditory	Visual	Speech	Concepts	Language	Emotional	Social	Disadvantaged	Spanish Version	Standard Scores	Inexpensive	Easy Scoring	Non-Verbal Cmprts.	OK Pre-School	Fast	Teacher Admin.	Group Test
Verbal Language Development Scale (0-1 to 16-0) extension of the communication portion of the Vineland Social Maturity Scale						+	+				rs	+	+	+	rs	+	+	+	
Vineland Social Maturity Scale (0-1 to adult) used to assess social maturity, competence and independence: self-help, self-direction, occupation, communication, locomotion and socialization	+					+	+	+	+		rs	+	+	+	rs	+	+	+	
Visual Analysis Test (5-0 to 7-0) ability to copy geometric designs as an indicator of children's overall visual-motor functioning		+		+							nv		+		+				
Walker Problem Behavior Identification Checklist (9-0 to 12-0) checklist to identify behavior problems: acting-out, withdrawal, distractibility, disturbed peer relations, immaturity								+	+		rs	cr	+	+	rs		+	+	

c = communication   cr = criterion referenced   ct = composite for several tests   exp = experimental edition

fs = appropriate for foreign speaking   ld = language disabled   nv = non-verbal   prs = parent rating scale   d/b = deaf/blind   rs = rating scale   sh = severely handicapped

Instrument, Item Content and CA Range	Group Test	Teacher Admin.	Fast	OK Pre-School	Non-Verbal Cmpnts.	Easy Scoring	Inexpensive	Standard Scores	Spanish Version	Disadvantaged	Social	Emotional	Language	Concepts	Speech	Visual	Auditory	Perceptual-Motor	Self-Help
Wepman Auditory Discrimination Tests (5-0 to 8-0) child indicates whether words are the same or different		+	+		+	+	+	cr									+		
Winterhaven Perceptual Forms Test (4-0 to 9-0) child copies geometric forms involving: actual reproduction, spatial orientation, organization and angulation	+	+	+	+	+	+	+		nv							+		+	
Yellow Brick Road (5-0 to 6-0) four batteries: motor, visual, auditory and language	+	+			+	+	+						+			+	+	+	

c = communication   cr = criterion referenced   ct = composite for several tests   exp = experimental edition

fs = appropriate for foreign speaking   ld = language disabled   nv = non-verbal   prs = parent rating scale   rs = rating scale   sh = severely handicapped

d/b = deaf/blind

Bibliography   153

BIBLIOGRAPHY

Adelman, H. S. "Learning problems, part I: An interaction view of cau-
sality." *Academic Therapy*, 6, 1970, 117-124.
Adelman, H. S. "The not so specific learning disabilities population."
Exceptional Children, 37, 1971, 528-533.
Albee, G. & Hamlin, R. "An investigation of the reliability and validity
of judgments of adjustment inferred from drawings." *Journal of
Clinical Psychology*, 1949, 5, 389-392.
Attwell, A., Orpet, R. & Meyers, C. E. "Kindergarten behavior ratings
as a predictor of academic achievement." *Journal of School Psy-
chology*, 6, 1967, 43-64.
Beatty, James R. "The analysis of an instrument for screening learning
disabilities." *Journal of Learning Disabilities*, 8, No. 3, March,
1975, 180-186.
Brofenbrenner, U. "Is early intervention effective?" In B. Z. Friedlander,
G. Sterritt & G. Kirk (Eds.), *Exceptional infant: Assessment and
intervention* Vol 3. New York: Brunner/Mazel, 1975.
Buros, O. K. (Ed.) *The fifth mental measurement yearbook*. Highland
Park, NJ: Gryphon, 1959.
Buros, O. K. (Ed.) *Reading tests and reviews*. Highland Park, NJ: Gry-
phon, 1968.
Buros, O. K. (Ed.) *The sixth mental measurement yearbook*. Highland
Park, NJ: Gryphon, 1965.
Buros, O. K. (Ed.) *The seventh mental measurement yearbook*. Highland
Park, NJ: Gryphon, 1972.
Camerm, N. "Individual and social factors in development of graphic
ability." *Journal of Psychology*, 1938, 5, 165-184.
Conrad, W. G. & Tobiessen, J. "The development of kindergarten be-
havior rating scales for the prediction of learning behavior disor-
ders." *Psychology in the Schools*, 4, 1967, 359-363.
Coury, J. P. & Nessa, D. B. "A screening method for early identification
of learning disabilities." Rev. Diss., University of Tennessee, 1973.
Davidson, J., Lichtenstein, R., Canter, A. & Cronin, P. *Project search:
Directory of developmental screening instruments*. Minneapolis:
Minneapolis Public Schools, 1977.

deHirsch, K., Jansky, J. & Langford, W. *Predicting reading failure: A preliminary study of reading, writing and spelling disabilities.* New York: Harper & Row, 1966.

Denhoff, E., Siqueland, M. L., Komich, M. P. & Hainsworth, P. K. "Developmental and predictive characteristics of items from the Meeting Street School Screening Test. *Developmental Medicine and Child Neurology*, 1968. 10, 220-232.

Dunn, L. (Ed.) *Exceptional children in the schools: Special education in transition* (2nd Ed.). New York: Holt, Rinehart & Winston, 1973.

Educational Testing Service. *Test collection.* Princeton, NJ: Educational Testing Service, 1971.

Erikson, Kai T. "Patient role and social uncertainty: A dilemma of the mentally ill." *Psychiatry,* 1957, 20, 263-274.

Fanning, P. "A new face on life." *National Observer.* October 19, 1974.

Faust, M. "Cognitive and language factors." In B. K. Keogh (Ed.) "Early identification of children with potential learning problems." *Journal of Special Education,* 4, 1970, 335-346.

Ferinden, W. E., Jr. & Jacobson, S. "Early identification of learning disabilities." *Journal of Learning Disabilities,* 3, No. 11, 1970, 589-593.

Feshbach, S., Adelman, H. & Fuller, W. W. "Early identification of children with high risk of reading failure." *Journal of Learning Disabilities,* 1974, 7, 639-644.

Frankenburg, W. K., Godkstein, A. & Camp, B. W. "The revised Denver Developmental Screening Test: Its accuracy as a screening instrument." *Journal of Pediatrics,* 79, 1971, 988-995.

Frankenburg, W. K., Camp, B. W. & VanNatta, P. A. "Reliability and stability of the Denver Developmental Screening Test." *Child Development,* 42, 1971, 1315.

Frankenburg, W. K., Camp, B. W. & VanNatta, P. A. "Validity of the Denver Developmental Screening Test." *Child Development,* 42, 1971, 475.

Frankenburg, W. K. & Camp, B. W. (Eds.) *Pediatric screening tests.* Springfield, IL: Charles C. Thomas, 1975.

Frankenburg, W. K., VanDoornirek, W. J., Lidell, T. N. & Dick, N. P. "The Denver Prescreening Developmental Questionnaire (PDQ)." *Pediatrics,* 1976, 57, 744-753.

Gardner, W. *Learning and behavior characteristics of exceptional children and youth.* Boston: Allyn & Bacon, 1977.

Goodenough, F. *Measurement and intelligence by drawings.* New York: Harcourt, Brace & World, 1926.

Goodenough, F. & Harris, D. *Goodenough-Harris Drawing Test.* New York: Harcourt, Brace & World, 1963.

Goodman, L. V. "A bill of rights for the handicapped." *American Education.* July, 1976.

Graubard, P. Children with behavioral disabilities. In L. M. Dunn (Ed.) *Exceptional children in the schools: Special education in transition* (2nd Ed.). New York: Holt, Rinehart & Winston, 1973.

Gray, S. & Klaus, R. "Experimental preschool programs for culturally deprived children." *Child Development,* 1965, 36, 887-898.

Guinan, J. & Hurley, J "An investigation on the reliability of human figure drawings. *Journal of Projective Techniques,* 1965, 29, 300-304.

Heber, R. & Garber, H. "The Milwaukee project: A study of the use of family intervention to prevent cultural familial mental retardation." In B. Z. Friedlander, G. Sterritt & G. Kirk (Eds.), *Exceptional infant: Assessment and intervention* (Vol. 3). New York: Brunner/Mazel, 1975.

Hill, J. "Models for screening." Minnesota University, Minneapolis: Institute of Child Development, 1970. (ERIC Document Reproduction Service No. ED 039 660)

Hoepfner, R., Stern, C. & Nummedal, S. (Eds.). *CSE-ECRC preschool/kindergarten test evaluations.* Los Angeles: UCLA Graduate School of Education, 1973.

Hornowski, B. *Studies on psychological development of children and youth by using children's drawings of a human figure.* Warsaw: Polskiej Akademic Nauk, 1970.

Hutton, J. B. "Relationship between teacher judgment, screening test data and academic performance for disadvantaged children." *Training School Bulletin,* 1972, 68, 197-201.

Ilg, F. & Ames, L. *School readiness: Behavior tests used at the Gesell Institute.* New York: Harper & Row, 1964.

Ireton, H. & Thwing, E. "Appraising the development of a preschool child by means of a standardized report prepared by the mother." *Clinical Pediatrics,* 1976, 15, 875-882.

Joiner, L. M. *A technical analysis of the variation in screening instruments and programs in New York State.* New York: Center for Advanced Study in Education, City University of New York, 1977.

Kapelis, L. "Early identification of reading failure: A comparison of two screening tests and teacher forecasts." *Journal of Learning Disabilities,* 1975, 8, 39-42.

Kaufman, A. S. & Kaufman, N. L. "Tests built from Piaget's and Gesell's tasks as predictors of first grade achievement." *Child Development,* 43, June, 1972, 521-535.

Kelly, G. R. "Group perceptual screening at first grade level." *Journal of Learning Disabilities,* 3, No. 12, Dec., 1970, 640-644.

Keogh, B. K. "The Bender-Gestalt as a predictive and diagnostic test of reading performance." *Journal of Consulting Psychology,* 29, 1965, 83-84.

Keogh, B. & Becker, L. "Early detection of learning problems: Questions, cautions, and guidelines." *Exceptional Children,* Sept., 1973, 5-11.

Keogh, B. K. & Smith, C. E. "Early identification of educationally high potential and high risk children." *Journal of School Psychology,* 8, 1970, 285-290.

Keogh, B. K. & Smith, C. E. "Group techniques and proposed scoring system for the Bender-Gestalt test with children." *Journal of Clinical Psychology,* 17, 1961, 172-175.

Kirk, S. A. *Educating exceptional children* (2nd Ed.). New York: Houghton-Mifflin, 1972.

Knobloch, H., Pasamanick, B. & Sherard, E. S. "A developmental screening inventory for infants." *Pediatrics,* 1966, 38, 1095-1108.

Koppitz, E. M., Mardis, V. & Stephens, T. "A note on screening school beginners with the Bender-Gestalt test." *Journal of Educational Psychology,* 52, 1961, 80-81.

Koppitz, E. M. *The Bender-Gestalt test for young children.* New York: Grune & Stratton, 1964.

Koppitz, E. M. *Psychological evaluation of children's human figure drawings.* New York: Grune & Stratton, 1968.

Landsman, M. & Dillard, H. *Evanston early identification scale.* Follett Education Corporation, 1967.

Lederman, E. & Blair, J. "Comparison of the level and predictive validity of Preschool Attainment Record ratings obtained from teachers and mothers." *Psychology in the Schools,* 1972, 9, 392-395.

Lerner, J. W. *Children with learning disabilities.* Boston: Houghton-Mifflin, 1976.

Lessler, K. "Health and educational screening of schoolage children: Definition and objectives." *American Journal of Public Health,* 1972, 191-198.

Machover, K. *Personality projection in the drawing of the human figure.* Springfield, IL: Charles C. Thomas, 1949.

Machover, S. *Cultural and racial variations in patterns of intellect.* New York: Contributions to Education, No. 875, 1943.

Maitland, S., Nadeau, J. B. E. & Nadeau, G. "Early screening practices." *Journal of learning disabilities,* 7, No. 10, Dec., 1974, 645-649.

Mardell, C. & Goldenberg, D. "For prekindergarten screening information: DIAL." *Journal of Learning Disabilities,* 8, No. 3, March, 1975, 140-147.

McCarthy, D. P. "The feasibility of a group Bender-Gestalt test for preschool and primary schoolaged children." *Journal of School Psychology,* 13, No. 2, 1975, 134-141.

Mecham, M. J., Jones, J. D. & Jex, J. L. "Use of the Utah Test of Language Development for screening language disabilities." *Journal of Learning Disabilities,* 1973, 6, 65-68.

Meier, J. *Screening and assessment of young children at developmental risk.* Washington, D. C.: DHEW Publication No. (05)73-90, March, 1973.

Mercer, J. *Labelling the mentally retarded, clinical and social system perspectives on mental retardation.* Berkeley, University of California Press, 1973.

Myklebust, H., et al. "Minimal brain damage in children, final report." Washington D. C.: DHEW, Division of Chronic Disease Programs, Neurological and Sensory Disease, 1970.

National Advisory Committee on the Handicapped. *The unfinished revolution: Education for the handicapped.* Washington D. C.: DHEW, 1976.

Norflett, M. A. "The Bender-Gestalt as a group screening instrument for first grade reading potential." *Journal of Learning Disabilities, 6,* No. 6, June/July, 1973, 383-388.

Ogdon, D. *Psychodiagnostics and personality assessment: A handbook* (2nd Ed.). Los Angeles: Western Psychological Services, 1976.

Pless, I. B., Snider, M., Eaton, A. E. & Kearsley, R. B. "A rapid screening test for intelligence in children." *American Journal of Diseases of Children,* 1965, 109, 533-537.

Powers, S. M. "The validity of the Vane Kindergarten Test in predicting achievement in kindergarten and first grade." *Educational and Psychological Measurement,* 1974, 34, 1003-1007.

Preschool test matrix: Individual test descriptions. Lexington, KY: University of Kentucky, Coordinating Office for Regional Resource Centers, March, 1976.

Proger, B. B. "Test review no. 3: Goldman-Fristoe-Woodcock Test of Auditory Discrimination." *Journal of Special Education,* 1970, 4, 367-373.

Proger, B. B. "Test review no. 9: Tests of basic experiences." *Journal of Special Education,* 1972, 6, 179-184.

Proger, B. B. "Test review no. 15: The pupil rating scale: Screening for learning disabilities." *Journal of Special Education,* 7, No. 3, Feb., 1973, 311-317.;

Resource Management Systems, Inc. (Carmel, California) "Finding kids with special needs: The background, development, field test and validation." 1977, 32 pages.;

Reynell, J. & Huntley, R. M. C. "New scales for the assessment of language development in young children." *Journal of Learning Disabilities,* 1971, 4, 549-557.

Reznikoff, M. & Toblen, D. "The use of human figure drawing in the diagnosis of organic pathology." *Journal of Consulting Psychology,* 1956, 20, 467-470.

Rivlin, H. N. (Ed.) *Encyclopedia of Modern Education.* Port Washington, NY: Kennikat Press, 1943.

Rogolsky, M. M. "Screening kindergarten children: A review and recommendations." *Journal of School Psychology,* 1968, 7, 18-27.

Rosner, J. *The Visual Analysis Test: An initial report.* Pittsburgh: University of Pittsburgh, Learning Research and Development Center, 1971.

Ross, Sterling L., Jr., DeYoung, H. G., & Cohen, J. S. "Confrontation: Special Education Placement and the Law." *Exceptional Children.* 1971 (September), 38, 1, 5-12.

Ruckhaber, C. "A technique of group administration of the Bender-Gestalt Test." *Psychology in the Schools,* Vol. 1, 1964, 53-56.

Rynders, J. E. & Horrobin, J. "Project EDGE: A communication stimulation program for Down's Syndrome infants." In B. Z. Friedlander, G. Sterritt & G. Kirk (Eds.) *Exceptional infant: Assessment and intervention* (Vol. 3). New York: Brunner/Mazel, 1975.

Salvia, J., Clark, G. M. & Ysseldyke, J. E. "Teacher Retention of Stereotypes of Exceptionality." *Exceptional Children,* 1973 (May), 37, 8, 651-652.

Schubert, D. "Decrease in rated adjustment on repeat DAP tests apparently due to lower motivation." *Journal of Projective Techniques and Personality Assessment,* 1969, 33-34.

Simon, A. & Joiner, L. "A Mexican version of the Peabody Picture Vocabulary Test." *Journal of Educational Measurement,* 1976, 13, 132-143.

Smith, C. E. & Keogh, B. K. "The group Bender-Gestalt as a reading readiness screening instrument." *Perceptual and Motor Skills,* 15, 1962, 639-645.

State University of New York. *A survey of educational screening programs in New York state school districts and boards of cooperative services.* Albany: The State Education Department, 1975.

Stevens, G. *A taxonomy of educational objectives for children with bodily disorders.* Pittsburgh: University of Pittsburgh Press, 1961.

Tarjan, G. In J. H. Meier (Ed.) *Screening and assessment of young children at developmental risk.* (The President's Committee on Mental Retardation, DHEW Publication No. (OS) 73-90). Washington D. C.: Government Printing Office, 1973.

Technical Assistance Development System. *Evaluation bibliography: Tadscript No. 2.* Chapel Hill, NC: University of North Carolina, 1973.

Thorpe, H. S. "Developmental screening of preschool children: A critical review of inventories used in health and educational programs." 53, No. 2, March, 1974, 362-370.

Uhitmyre, J. "The significance of artistic excellance in the judgment of and adjustment inferred from human figure drawings." *Journal of Consulting Psychology*, 1953, 17, 421-424.

VanDeRiet, V. & Resnick, M. *A sequential approach to early childhood and elementary education.* Washington, D. C.: DHEW, Division of Research and Evaluation, Office of Child Development, 1973.

Vane, J. & Eisen, V. "The Goodenough Draw-A-Man Test and signs of maladjustment in kindergarten children." *Journal of Clinical Psychology*, 1962, 18, 276-279.

Vane, J. R. "The Vane Kindergarten Test." *Journal of Clinical Psychology*, 1968, 24, 121-154.

Webb, W. W. & Pate, J. E. "Predicting failure in the primary grades." *Educational and Psychological Measurement*, 1970, 30, 459-462.

Weikart, D. P. "Relationship of curriculum, teaching, and learning in preschool education." In J. C. Stanley (Ed.) *Preschool programs for the disadvantaged: Five experimental approaches to early childhood education.* Baltimore: John Hopkins, 1972.

Whitmyre, J. W. "The significance of artistic excellence on the judgement of adjustment inferred from human figure drawings." *Journal of Consulting Psychology*, 1953, 17, 421-424.

APPENDIX:
SCREENING INSTRUMENT INVENTORY

The ABC Inventory (1965)
(N. Adair and G. Glesch)
 Specimen set ($2.00)
 Set of 50 ($5.90)
 Per pupil cost ($.10)

Research Concepts
1368 East Airport Road
Muskegon, Michigan 49444

Adaptive Behavior Scales (1975)
(N. Nihira, R. Foster, M. Shellhas and H. Leland)
 Initial materials ($5.00)
 Public school version ($7.00)
 Per pupil cost ($1.00)

American Association on Mental Deficiency
5201 Connecticut Avenue, NW
Washington, D.C. 20015

American School Reading Readiness Test (1964)
(W. E. Pratt and G. A. W. Stouffer)
 Specimen set ($1.10)
 Set of 35 ($5.90)
 Per pupil cost ($.40)

Bobbs-Merrill Co., Inc.
Test Division
4300 West 62nd Street
Indianapolis, Indiana 46206

**Anton Brenner Developmental Gestalt Test
of School Readiness (1964)**
(A. Brenner)

Kit ($13.50)
Per pupil cost ($.26)

Western Psychological Services
12031 Wilshire Boulevard
Los Angeles, California 90025

Arizona Articulation Proficiency Scale: Revised (1970)
(J. B. Fudala)

Kit ($18.50)
Per pupil cost ($.26)

Western Psychological Services
12031 Wilshire Boulevard
Los Angeles, California 90025

**Assets: A Survey of Student's Educational Talents and Skills
(1978)**
(Grand Rapids, Michigan Public Schools)

Specimen set ($4.95)
Teacher Survey Form
Parent Survey Form
Student Survey Form
Early Elementary
Later Elementary
Student Profile Record Form
Administrators Manual
Set of 35 ($29.10)
Per pupil cost ($.70, in quantity)

Learning Publications, Inc.
PO Box 1326, Department A
Holmes Beach, Florida 33509

Bankson Language Screening Test (1977)
(N. W. Bankson)

Set ($14.95)
Per pupil cost ($.20)

University Park Press
Chamber of Commerce Building
Baltimore, Maryland 21202

Basic Concept Inventory (1967)
(S. E. Engelmann)

Kit ($30.00)
Per pupil cost ($.33)

Follett Publishing Company
1010 W. Washington Boulevard
Chicago, Illinois 60607

Basic School Skills Inventory (1975)
(L. Goodman and D. Hammill)

Specimen set ($2.10)
Kit ($12.00)
Per pupil cost ($.05)

Follett Publishing Company
1010 W. Washington Boulevard
Chicago, Illinois 60607

Bayley Scales of Infant Development (1969)
(N. Bayley)

Initial Materials and set of 25 ($98.00)
Per pupil cost ($.25)

Psychological Corporation
304 East 45th Street
New York, New York 10017

Bender Motor Gestalt Test (1964)
(L. Bender)

Prototype ($2.50)

American Orthopsychiatric Association
1790 Broadway
New York, New York 10019

Birth-Three Scale (1977)
(T. E., Bangs, and S. Garrett)

Learning Concepts
2501 North Lamar
Austin, Texas 78705

Boehm Test of Basic Concepts (1969)
(A. E. Boehm)

Specimen set ($1.50)
Set of 30 ($7.75)
Per pupil cost ($.24)

Psychological Corporation
304 East 45th Street
New York, New York 10017

Boyd Developmental Progress Scale (1974)
(R. D. Boyd)

Initial materials ($12.00)
Per pupil cost ($.03)

Inland Counties Regional Center, Inc.
San Bernardino, California 92408

Burks Behavior Rating Scale (1969)
(H. Burks)

Set of 25 ($3.85)
Per pupil cost ($.15)

Arden Press
Huntington Beach, California 91734

Cain-Levine Social Competency
(L. F. Cain, S. Levine, and F. F. Elzey)

Specimen set ($1.75)
Set of 25 ($6.00)
Per pupil cost ($.16)

Consulting Psychologists Press, Inc.
577 College Avenue
Palo Alto, California 94306

Camelot Behavioral Checklist (1974)

Camelot Behavioral Systems
PO Box 607
Parsons, Kansas 67357

Carolina Developmental Profile (1975)
(D. L. Lillie and G. L. Harbin)

Technical Assistance Development System (TADS)
803 Churchill
Chapel Hill, North Carolina 27514

Carrow Elicited Language Inventory (1974)
(E. Carrow)

Kit ($39.95)
Per pupil cost ($.18)

Learning Concepts
2501 North Lamar
Austin, Texas 78705

CCD Developmental Progress Scale (Experimental Form) (1969)

Hardbound manual, 20 copies of scale ($12.00)

Inland Counties Regional Center, Inc.
PO Box 6127
San Bernardino, California 92408

Child Behavior Rating Scale (1962)
(R. N. Cassel)

Set of 25 ($7.50)
Per pupil cost ($.26)

Western Psychological Services
12031 Wilshire Boulevard
Los Angeles, California 90025

Children's Self-Social Construct Tests
(Experimental Version) — Preschool Level (1964)
(E. H. Henderson, B. H. Long, and R. C. Ziller)

Specimen set ($6.00)
Set ($8.00)
Per pupil cost ($.06)

Virginia Research Associates, Ltd.
PO Box 5501
Charlottesville, Virginia

Cincinatti Autonomy Test Battery
(T. J. Banta, and T. S. Banta)

T. S. Banta
University of Cincinatti
Cincinatti, Ohio 45221

Circus (1974)
(S. B. Anderson, G. A. Bogatz, T. W. Draper, A. Jungeblut, G. Sidwell, W. C. Ward, and A. Yates)

Specimen Set ($5.00)
Kit ($63.00)
Per pupil cost ($1.25)

Educational Testing Service
Princeton, New Jersey 08540

Cognitive Skills Assessment Battery (1974)
(A. E. Boehm and B. R. Slater)

Specimen set ($1.50)
Kit ($17.50)
Per pupil cost ($.16)

Teachers College Press
Columbia University
1234 Amsterdam Avenue
New York, New York 10027

Columbia Mental Maturity Scale (1972)
(R. Burgemeister, L. H. Blum and I. Lorge)

Kit ($50.00)

Harcourt, Brace & World, Inc.
757 Third Avenue
New York, New York 10017

Communicative Evaluation Chart from Infancy to Five Years (1963)
(R. M. Andersen, M. Miles and P. A. Matheny)

Per pupil cost ($.25)

Educators Publishing Service
75 Moulton Street
Cambridge, Massachusetts 02138

Comprehensive Identification Process (CIP) (1976)
(R. R. Zehrbach)

Kit ($59.95)
Per pupil cost ($.70)

Scholastic Testing Service, Inc.
480 Meyer Road
Bensenville, Illinois 60106

Contemporary School Readiness Test (1970)
(C. E. Sauer)

Manual and scoring keys ($1.50)
Per pupil cost ($.25)

Montana Reading Publications
225 Stapleton Building
Billings, Montana 59101

Cooperative Preschool Inventory (1970)
(B. M. Caldwell)

Specimen set ($3.00)
Set ($5.50)
Per pupil cost ($.15)

Educational Testing Services
Princeton, New Jersey 18540

Dailey Language Facility Test (1966)
(J. T. Dailey)

Test and instructions ($15.00)

The Allington Corporation
801 North Pitt Street
Alexandria, Virginia 22314

Del Rio Language Screening Test (1975)
(S. A. Toronto, D. Leverman, C. Hanna, P. Rosenzweig and A. Maldonado)

Kit ($9.00)
Per pupil cost ($.06)

National Educational Laboratory Publishers, Inc.
PO Box 1003
Austin, Texas 78767

Denver Articulation Screening Exam (DASE) (1973)
(A. F. Drumwright)

Initial materials ($6.85)
Per pupil cost ($.02)

A. F. Drumwright
East 51st Avenue and Lincoln Street
Denver, Colorado 80216

Denver Developmental Screening Test (1970)
(W. K. Frankenburg and J. B. Dobbs)

Initial materials ($25.00)
Per pupil cost ($.02)

Ladoca Project & Publishing Foundation, Inc.
East 51st Avenue and Lincoln Street
Denver, Colorado 80216

Denver Prescreening Developmental Questionnaire (1974)
(W. K. Frankenburg)

Initial materials ($15.00)
Per pupil cost ($.03)

Ladoca Project & Publishing Foundation, Inc.
East 51st Avenue and Lincoln Street
Denver, Colorado 80216

Detroit Tests of Learning Aptitude (1959)
(H. J. Baker and B. Leland)

Sample packet ($10.80)
Kit ($20.15)
Per pupil cost ($.21)

Bobbs-Merrill Company
4300 West 64th Street
Indianapolis, Indiana 46206

Developmental Guidelines
(C. C. Sprugel and S. Goldberg)

University of Illinois
College of Education
Institute for Child Behavior and Development
Urbana, Illinois 61801

**Developmental Indicator for the
Assessment of Learning (DIAL) (1972)**
(C. Mardell and D. Goldenberg)

Kit ($99.50)
Per pupil cost ($.75)

DIAL, Inc.
PO Box 911
Highland Park, Illinois 60035

Developmental Key for Assessing Children's Growth (1974)

Frank Porter Graham Child Development Center
Early Childhood Section
University of North Carolina
Chapel Hill, North Carolina 27514

Developmental Profile (1972)
(C. D. Alpern and T. J. Ball)

Kit ($11.30)
Per pupil cost ($.20)

Psychological Development Publications
PO Box 3198
Aspen, Colorado 81611

Developmental Screening Inventory (DSI) (1966)
(H. Knobloch)

Set of 25 ($4.50)
Per pupil cost ($.18)

Department of Pediatrics
Albany Medical College
Albany, New York 12208

Developmental Test of Visual Motor Integration (1967)
(K. Beery and N. Buktenica)

Specimen set ($2.10)
Complete set ($36.00)
Per pupil cost ($.45 – short form; $.63 – long form)

Follett Publishing Company
1010 West Washington Boulevard
Chicago, Illinois 60607

Developmental Test of Visual Perception (1966)
(M. Frostig)

Specimen set ($5.00)
Examiner's Kit ($10.00)
Per pupil cost ($.40)

Consulting Psychologists Press
577 College Avenue
Palo Alto, California 94306

**Early Childhood Assessment: A Criterion-Referenced
Screening Device (1973)**
(R. Wendt, R. Schramm and D. Schmaltz)

Initial materials ($8.00)
Per pupil cost ($.25)

Cooperative Educational Service Agency 13
908 West Main Street
Waupun, Wisconsin 53963

Early Detection Inventory (1967)
(F. E. McGahan and G. McGahan)

Initial materials ($8.25)
Per pupil cost ($.55)

Follett Publishing Company
1010 West Washington Boulevard
Chicago, Illinois 60607

**Early Education Screening Test –
Battery of Basic Skills Development (1969)**
(T. J. Mayer)

School District of University City
University City, Missouri 63130

Early Identification Screening Inventory
(E. Medvedeff)

Specimen set ($3.25)
Kit ($8.50)
Per pupil cost ($.15)

Mark James Press
1568 West Exchange Street
Akron, Ohio 44313

The Educational Developmental Program, Kit I (1970)
(W. Peterson)

Kit ($89.95)
Per pupil cost ($.75)

Special Child Publications, Inc.
4535 Union Bay Place, NE
Seattle, Washington 98105

Eliot-Pearson Screening Inventory (1976)
(S. J. Meisels and M. S. Wiske)

Eliot-Person / Department of Child Study
Tufts University
105 College Avenue
Medford, Massachusetts 02155

Evanston Early Identification Scale
(Field Research Edition) (1967)
(M. Landsman and H. Dilliard)

Initial materials ($3.09)
Per pupil cost ($.10)

Follett Publishing Company
1010 West Washington Boulevard
Chicago, Illinois 60607

Fairview Behavior Evaluation Battery
for the Mentally Retarded (1971)
(R. T. Ross, M. A. Boroskin and J. S. Giampiccolo)

Specimen set ($3.00)
Kit ($52.00)
Per pupil cost ($.10)

Research Department — Fairview State Hospital
2501 Harbor Boulevard
Costa Mesa, California 92626

First Grade Screening Test (FGST) (1966)
(J. E. Pate and W. W. Webb)

Specimen set ($2.50)
Kit ($14.50)
Per pupil cost ($.24)

American Guidance Service, Inc.
Publishers' Building
Circle Pines, Minnesota 55014

A General Screening Instrument
(W. J. Harris and D. R. King)

University of Maine
Department of Special Education
Shibles Hall
Orono, Maine

Gessell Developmental Examination (1965)
(F. Ilg and L. B. Ames)

Set ($12.50)
Per pupil cost ($.33)

Western Psychological Services
Programs for Education
PO Box 85
Lumberville, Pennsylvania

Gessell Developmental Schedules (1940)
(A. Gessell)

Mr. Nigel Cox
69 Fawn Drive
Cheshire, Connecticut 06410

Goldman-Fristoe-Woodcock Auditory Skills Test Battery (1969)
(R. Goldman, M. Fristoe and R. Woodcock)

Complete kit ($23.00)
Per pupil cost ($.07)

American Guidance Service, Inc.
Publishers' Building
Circle Pines, Minnesota 55014

Goodenough Harris Drawing Test (1963)
(S. L. Goodenough and D. B. Harris)

Initial materials ($5.72)
Per pupil cost ($.25)

Harcourt, Brace, Jovanovich, Inc.
757 Third Avenue
New York, New York 10017

Harris Tests of Lateral Dominance (1958)
(A. J. Harris)

Specimen set ($1.75)
Set ($8.40)
Per pupil cost ($.13)

The Psychological Corporation
304 East 45th Street Street
New York, New York 10017

Houston Test for Language Development (1963)
(M. Grabtree)

Kit ($35.00)

Houston Test Company
PO Box 35152
Houston, Texas

Infant Behavior Inventory (1975)
(E. Shaefer and M. Aaronson)
National Institute of Mental Health
Rockville, Maryland

Infant Intelligence Scale (1960)
(P. Cattell)
Kit and Manual ($119.00)
Per pupil cost ($.12)
Psychological Corporation
304 East 45th Street
New York, New York 10017

Initial Screening Checklist (1977)
(W. J. Harris)
Per pupil cost ($.15)
Walter J. Harris
Shibles Hall
University of Maine
Orono, Maine 04473

Inter-American Services: Test of General Ability, Preschool Level (1966)
Kit ($6.00)
Per pupil cost ($.06)
Guidance Testing Associates
6516 Shirley Avenue
Austin, Texas 78752

Inventory for Language Abilities (1972)
(E. H. Minskoff, D. E. Wiseman and J. C. Minskoff)
Educational Performance Associates
Ridgefield, New Jersey 07657

Inventory of Readiness Skills (1973)
(J. Shelquist, B. Breeze and B. Jacquot)

Specimen set ($4.65)
Set ($10.95)
Per pupil cost ($.37)

Educational Programmers, Inc.
PO Box 332
Roseburg, Oregon 97470

Jansky Screening Index (1972)
(J. J. Jansky)

Initial materials ($16.50)
Per pupil cost ($.04)

Matt-Jansky
120 East 89th Street
New York, New York 10028

Kindergarten Auditory Screening Test (1971)
(J. Katz)

Specimen set $2.10
Kit – record and guide ($7.50)
Per pupil cost ($.27)

Follett Publishing Company
1010 West Washington Boulevard
Chicago, Illinois 60607

Kindergarten Evaluation of Learning Potential (KELP) (1969)
(J. A. R. Wilson and N. C. Robeck)

Set ($219.36)

Aevac, Inc.
1500 Park Avenue
South Plainfield, New Jersey 07080

Language Facility Test (1965)
(J. T. Daily)

Initial materials ($15.00)

Allington Corporation
801 North Pitt Street
Alexandria, Virginia 22314

**Language and Learning Disorders of the
Pre-Academic Child (1968)**
(T. E. Bangs)

Kit (12.75)

Western Psychological Services
12031 Wilshire Boulevard
Los Angeles, California 90025

Laradon Articulation Scale (1963)
(W. Edmonston)

Kit ($32.50)
Per pupil cost ($.19)

Western Psychological Services
12031 Wilshire Boulevard
Los Angeles, California 90025

Lexington Developmental Scale (Short Form) (1975)
*(Child Development Centers of United Cerebral Palsy
of the Bluegrass)*

Short Form — manual and chart ($1.75)
Per pupil cost ($.25)

United Cerebral Palsy of the Bluegrass, Inc.
PO Box Springhill Drive
Lexington, Kentucky 40503

The Magic Kingdom: A Preschool Screening Program (1973)
(W. Gingold)

Kit ($39.00)
Per pupil cost ($4.00)

Southeast Mental Health and Retardation Center
700 1st Avenue South
Fargo, North Dakota 58102

A Manual for the Assessment of a "Deaf-Blind,"
Multiple Handicapped Child — Revised Edition
(M. T. Collins and J. M. Rudolph)

Midwest Regional Resource Center for
Services to Deaf-Blind Children
PO Box 420
Lansing, Michigan 48902

Maturity Level for School Entrance
and Reading Readiness (1959)
(K. M. Banham)

Specimen set ($.65)
Set ($4.50)
Per pupil cost ($.08)

American Guidance Service, Inc.
Publishers' Building
Circle Pines, Minnesota 55014

Maxfield-Bucholz Scale of Social Maturity
with Pre-School (1958)
(K. E. Maxfield)

Book and record blank ($3.00)
Per pupil cost ($.15)

American Foundation for the Blind, Inc.
15 West 16th Street
New York, New York 10011

Meeting Street School Screening Test (1969)
(P. K. Hainsworth and M. L. Siqueland)
   Set ($12.00)
   Per pupil cost ($.10)
Meeting Street School
667 Waterman Avenue
East Providence, RI   02914

Memory-for-Designs Test (1960)
(F. K. Graham and B. S. Kendall)
   Initial materials ($17.00)
Psychological Test Specialties
PO Box 1441
Missoula, Montana

Memphis Comprehensive Developmental Scale (1973)
   Set ($1.50)
Lear Siegler, Inc. / Fearson
Belmont, California

Minnesota Child Development Inventory (1972)
(H. R. Ireton and E. J. Thwing)
   Specimen set ($6.00)
   Complete set ($45.00)
   Per pupil cost ($.15)
Behavior Science Systems, Inc.
PO Box 1108
Minneapolis, Minnesota 55440

Missouri Children's Picture Series (1963)
(J. Sines, J. Pauker and L. Sines)
   Kit ($25.00)
   Per pupil cost ($.16)
Psychological Assessment and Services, Inc.
PO Box 1031
Iowa City, Iowa 52240

Motor Free Visual Perception Test (1972)
(R. P. Colarusso and D. D. Hammill)

Set ($17.50)
Per pupil cost ($.06)

Academic Therapy Publications
1539 Fourth Street
San Rafael, California 94901

Motor Problems Inventory (1972)
(G. D. Riley)

Kit ($9.50)
Per pupil cost ($.85)

Western Psychological Services
12031 Wilshire Boulevard
Los Angeles, California 90025

Move-Grow-Learn (Movement Skills Survey) (1971)
(R. E. Orpet and L. L. Heustis)

Kit ($17.28)
Per pupil cost ($.20)

Follett Publishing Company
1010 West Washington Boulevard
Chicago, Illinois 60607

Northwestern Syntax Screening Test (1969)
(L. Lee)

Set ($10.00)
Per pupil cost ($.20)

Dr. Laura Lee
Northwestern University
Evanston, Illinois 60201

Oseretsky Test of Motor Proficiency (1946)
(E. A. Doll)

Kit ($35.00)
Per pupil cost ($.08)

American Guidance Services, Inc.
Publishers' Building
Circle Pines, Minnesota 55014

Parent Readiness Evaluation of Preschoolers (PREP) (1968)
(A. E. Ahr)

Manual and test booklet ($2.40)
Per pupil cost ($.22)

Priority Innovations, Inc.
PO Box 792
Skokie, Illinois 60076

Photo Articulation Test (1969)
(K. Pendergest, S. E. Dickey, J. W. Selmar and A. L. Soder)

Initial materials ($14.75)

Interstate Printers and Publishers
19-27 North Jackson Street
Danville, Illinois 61832

Piers-Harris Children's Self-Concept Scale (1969)

Set ($2.25)

Counselor Recordings and Tests
PO Box 6184
Acklen Station
Nashville, Tennessee 37213

Pre-Academic Learning Inventory (1975)
(M. H. Wood and F. M. Layne)

Initial materials ($16.50)
Per pupil cost ($.30)

Educational Dimensions, Ltd.
PO Box 366
Cedar Falls, Iowa 50613

Predictive Screening Test of Articulation (1968)
(Van Riper and Erickson)

Initial investment ($1.00)

Division of Continuing Education
Western Michigan University
Kalamazoo, Michigan 49008

Preprimary Profile (Introduction to My Child) (1966)
(J. H. Schiff and M. I. Friedman)

Kit ($11.00)
Per pupil cost ($.44)

Science Research Associates
259 East Erie Street
Chicago, Illinois 60611

Pre-Reading Screening Procedures (1977)
(B. H. Slingerland)

Specimen set ($3.00)
Set ($14.50)
Per pupil cost ($.58)

Educators Publishing Service, Inc.
75 Moulton Street
Cambridge, Massachusetts 02138

**Preschool Behavior Questionnaire: Manual and
Questionnaire Set (1974)**
(L. Behar)

Initial materials ($4.00)
Per pupil cost ($.08)

LINC Press
1006 Lamond Avenue
Durham, North Carolina 27701

Preschool Language Scale (1969)
(I. L. Zimmerman, V. G. Steiner and R. L. Evatt)

Set ($15.00
Per pupil cost ($.65)

Charles E. Merrill Publishing Company
1300 Alum Creek Drive
Columbus, Ohio 43216

Preschool Screening Survey
(C. W. Beers)

Kit ($20.00)
Per pupil cost ($1.00)

Clifford W. Beers Guidance Clinic
The Celentano School
400 Conner Street
New Haven, Connecticut 06511

Preschool Screening System
(P. Hainsworth and R. Hainsworth)

Set of 50 ($16.00)
Per pupil cost ($.16)

Hainsworth & Hainsworth
Early Recognition Intervention System
PO Box 1635
Pawtucket, Rhode Island 02862

Primary Academic Sentiment Scale (1968)
(G. R. Thompson)

Specimen set ($3.50)
Set of 35 ($29.00)
Per pupil cost ($.90)

Priority Innovations, Inc.
PO Box 792
Skokie, Illinois 60076

Primary Self-Concept Inventory (1973)
(D. Muller and R. Leonetti)

Specimen set ($5.15)
Set ($10.10)
Per pupil cost ($.60)

Learning Concepts, Inc.
2501 North Lamar
Austin, Texas 78705

Progressive Assessment Charts of Social Development:
Form I (Third Edition) and Form II (Second Edition) (1962)

Initial materials ($7.50)
Per pupil cost ($.08)

NAMH
39 Queen Anne Street West 1
London, England

Purdue Perceptual Motor Survey (1966)
(E. G. Roach and N. C. Kephart)

Initial Materials ($16.45)

Charles E. Merrill Publishing Company
1300 Alum Creek Drive
Columbus, Ohio 43216

Quick Neurological Screening Test (1977)
(H. M. Sterling, M. Mutti, N. V. Spalding and C. S. Crawford)
  Initial materials ($12.00)
  Per pupil cost ($.18)
Academic Therapy Publications
PO Box 899
1539 Fourth Street
San Rafael, California 94901

Quick Screening Scale of Mental Development (1963)
(K. M. Banham)
  Specimen set ($2.00)
  Per pupil cost ($.14)
Psychometric Affiliates
PO Box 3167
Munster, Indiana 46321

Quick Test (1962)
(R. B. Ammons and C. H. Ammons)
  Set ($16.00)
  Per pupil cost ($.10)
Psychological Test Specialists
PO Box 1441
Missoula, Montana 59801

Quick Word Test (1967)
(E. F. Borgatta)
  Initial materials ($1.50)
  Per pupil cost ($.11)
Harcourt, Brace, Jovanovich, Inc.
757 Third Avenue
New York, New York 10017

Rapid Developmental Screening Checklist (1972)

American Academy of Pediatrics
Chapter 3, District II
New York, New York

Receptive-Expressive Emergent Language Scale (REEL) (1972)
(K. R. Bzoch and R. League)

Initial materials ($16.50)
Per pupil cost ($.30)

Tree of Life Press
1329 NE Second Street
PO Box 447
Gainesville, Florida

Reynell Developmental Language Scales (1969)
(J. Reynell)

Set of 25 ($60.00)
Per pupil cost ($3.80)

Neer Publishing Company, Ltd.
2 Jennings Building
Thames Avenue
Windsor Berks SL 41 QS England

Riley Articulation and Language Test
(G. D. Riley)

Kit ($7.50)
Per pupil cost ($.30)

Western Psychological Services
12031 Wilshire Boulevard
Los Angeles, California 90025

Riley Preschool Developmental Screening Inventory (1969)
(C. M. D. Riley)

   Kit ($7.50)
   Per pupil cost ($.30)

Western Psychological Services
12031 Wilshire Boulevard
Los Angeles, California 90025

Rosner Perceptual Survey (1969)
(J. Rosner)

Learning Research and Development Center
University of Pittsburgh
Pittsburgh, Pennsylvania

Rosner-Richman Perceptual Survey (1969)
(J. Rosner and V. Richman)

Learning Research and Development Center
University of Pittsburgh
Pittsburgh, Pennsylvania

School Entrance Checklist (1969)
(J. McLeod)

   Set ($1.75)
   Per pupil cost ($.20)

Educator's Publishing Service
75 Moulton Street
Cambridge, Massachusetts   02138

School Readiness Checklist — Ready or Not (1968)
(J. J. Austin and J. C. Lafferty)

   Initial materials ($4.95)
   Per pupil cost ($.12)

Research Concepts
1368 East Airport Road
Muskegon, Michigan   49444

School Readiness Survey (1975)
(F. L. Jordan and J. Massey)

Survey and manual ($1.00)
Per pupil cost ($.50)

Consulting Psychologists Press, Inc.
577 College Avenue
Palo Alto, California 94306

Screening Test of Academic Readiness (STAR) (1966)
(A. E. Ahr)

Specimen set ($3.50)
Kit ($29.00)
Per pupil cost ($.86)

Priority Innovations, Inc.
PO Box 792
Skokie, Illinois 60076

Screening Test for the Assignment of Remedial Treatment (START) (1968)
(A. E. Ahr)

Specimen set ($3.50)
Kit ($29.00)
Per pupil cost ($.85)

Priority Innovations, Inc.
PO Box 792
Skokie, Illinois 60076

Screening Test for Auditory Comprehension of Language (1973)
(E. Carrow-Woolfolk)

Manual and booklet ($4.75)
Per pupil cost ($.80)

Learning Concepts
2501 North Lamar
Austin, Texas 78705

Sequenced Inventory of Communication Development (1975)
(D. L. Hedrick, E. M. Prather and A. R. Tobin)

Kit ($95.00)

University of Washington Press
Seattle, Washington 98105

Slingerland Screening Tests for Identifying Children with Specific Language Disability (1974)
(B. H. Slingerland)

Forms A, B, C and D ($29.50)
Per pupil cost ($.30)

Educators Publishing Service, Inc.
75 Moulton Street
Cambridge, Massachusetts 02138

Southern California Perceptual-Motor Tests (1968)
(A. J. Ayres)

Kit ($15.50)
Per pupil cost ($.10)

Western Psychological Services
12031 Wilshire Boulevard
Los Angeles, California 90025

Specific Language Disability Test (1968)
(N. Malcomesius)

Initial materials ($3.75)
Per pupil cost ($.34)

Educators Publishing Service, Inc.
75 Moulton Street
Cambridge, Massachusetts 02138

Sprigle School Readiness Screening Test (1965)
(Psychological Clinic and Research Center)

Specimen set ($5.00)
Kit ($18.00)
Per pupil cost ($.70)

Learning to Learn School, Inc.
1936 San Marco Boulevard
Jacksonville, Florida 32207

The TARC Assessment System (1975)
(W. Sailor and B. J. Mix)

Set ($5.95)
Per pupil cost ($.04)

H & H Enterprises, Inc.
PO Box 3342
Lawrence, Kansas 66044

Templin-Darley Tests of Articulation (1969)
(M. C. Templin and F. L. Darley)

Specimen set ($5.75)
Per pupil cost ($.10)

Bureau of Educational Research and Service (Extension Div.)
C-20 East Hall
University of Iowa
Iowa City, Iowa 52242

Test of Basic Experiences (1975)
(M. H. Moss)

Initial investment ($88.00) ($44.00 each level)
Per pupil cost ($.60)

CTB/McGraw Hill
Del Norte Research Park
Monterey, California 93940

Test of Nonverbal Auditory Discrimination (TENVAD) (1975)
(N. A. Buktenica)

Specimen set ($2.10)
Set ($11.75)
Per pupil cost ($.12)

Follett Publishing Company
1010 West Washington Boulevard
Chicago, Illinois 60607

Utah Test of Language Development (1967)
(M. J. Mecham, J. L. Jex and J. D. Jones)

Set ($25.00)
Per pupil cost ($.10)

Communication Research Associates, Inc.
PO Box 11012
Salt Lake City, Utah 84147

Vane Kindergarten Test (1968)
(J. R. Vane)

Set ($7.50)
Per pupil cost ($.07)

Clinical Psychology Publishing Company, Inc.
4 Conant Square
Brandon, Vermont 05733

Verbal Language Development Scale (1971)
(M. J. Mecham)

Specimen set ($1.00)
Kit ($3.25)
Per pupil cost ($.10)

American Guidance Services, Inc.
Publishers' Building
Circle Pines, Minnesota 55014

Vineland Social Maturity Scale (1965)
(E. A. Doll)

Initial materials ($4.80)
Per pupil cost ($.12)

American Guidance Service, Inc.
Publishers' Building
Circle Pines, Minnesota 55014

Visual Analysis Test (1971)
(J. Rosner)

Initial materials ($1.00)

Learning Research and Development Center
University of Pittsburgh
Pittsburgh, Pennsylvania

Walker Problem Behavior Identification Checklist (1970)
(H. M. Walker)

Kit ($9.50)
Per pupil cost ($.09)

Western Psychological Services
12031 Wilshire Boulevard
Los Angeles, California 90025

Wepman Auditory Discrimination Tests (1973)
(J. M. Wepman)

Manual and forms ($8.50)
Per pupil cost ($.14)

Language Research Association
175 East Delaware Place
Chicago, Illinois 60611

Winterhaven Perceptual Forms Test (1963)

Lion's Club
PO Box 111
Winterhaven, Florida 33880

Yellow Brick Road (1975)
(C. Kallstrom)

Kit ($39.95)
Per pupil cost ($.10)

Learning Concepts
2501 North Lamar
Austin, Texas 78705

196   *Identifying Children with Special Needs*

Koppitz, E. M., 102, 105
Kirk, S. A., 69
Landsman, M., 103
Law, 19
  Public Law 94-142, 20, 77
Learning impediments, 13
Least restrictive alternative, 26
Locally designed instruments, 43
Machover, K., 102
Machover, S., 104
Maitland, S., 31
Measurement utility, 89
Mental measurement, 88
Mental Measurement Yearbook, 90, 99
Metropolitan Readiness Test, 45, 101
National Advisory Committee on the Handicapped, 1, 2
National Education Project, 22
Nadeau, G., 31
Nadeau, J. B. E., 31
Non-verbal components, 114
Normed Technical Excellence, 90
Nummedal, S., 89
Observation process, 12, 13
Ogden, D., 102
Outreach programs, 47
Peabody Picture Vocabulary Test, 45, 92
Pediatric Screening Tests, 88
Placement recommendations, 14
Procedural safeguards, 61
Programming,
  Criterion-referenced based, 75

Reading tests, 88
Referral, 7-9, 59, 60
Reliability, 106
Riley Preschool Development Inventory, 108
Rivlin, H. N., 71
Ross, S. L., 25
Salvia, J., 24
School programming, 29
Schubert, D., 103
Screening,
  comprehensive, 38
  drawing conclusions, 12
  early, 3-5
  fixed, 41
  formal, 6, 7
  four basic features, 11, 12
  medical model, 74
  parents and, 49
  programs, 33
  reliability, 87
  resistence to, 12
  selective, 38
  sources of bias-error, 80-85
  systematic, 12
  unintended meanings, 15
  validity, 85
Second-level screening, 94
Secondary deficits, 14
Self-fulfilling prophecy, 17, 74
Sensory-motor deficits, 3
Sensory-motor maturation, 102
Sensc.y-motor skills, 3
Severity of problems, 30, 31
Simon, A., 91